Home, Sweet Motorhome

Life Lessons from a Half-Century of RVing

Gaylord Maxwell

LIFE ON WHEELS, INC.

First Printing: June, 2003

ISBN: 0-9741961-1-8

Published by Life on Wheels, Inc.
P.O. Box 9755
Moscow, Idaho 83843
www.lifeonwheels.com

Cover design by Robert S. Tinnon
Cover photograph taken near Yuma, Arizona, by Tom Brownold
Interior design by Robert S. Tinnon Design

Production services by Rena J. Copperman and Maxye Henry

Additional copies may be obtained from

Gaylord Maxwell
1471 Mica Mountain Road
Deary, Idaho 83823

Please send $14.95 plus $4.50 shipping and handling.

Dedicated to my kids—
Sherry, Lee, and Mary Jane—
who often don't know where we are.

Contents

■ ■ ■

Preface

This book is my response to the people who have asked me to publish a collection of my columns from *MotorHome* magazine. They began in January of 1981 and have appeared every month since, except for one month in 1991 when our motorhome burned up with all our possessions, including my computer. Actually, this collection dates back only to 1991 because of space limitations for this book.

I tried to categorize the columns into chapters or themed groups, but was unsuccessful. The result is bits and pieces of opinions and ideas about motorhomes and life in general as they comprise a lifestyle, laid out in more or less chronological order. More than thirty years of travel in all forty-eight contiguous states, as well as in several Canadian provinces and Mexican states—in all, some half-million miles—in thirteen different motorhomes, has taken us to many beautiful and exciting places. We've spent well over half of three decades in motorhomes, and, although I don't profess to know it all, I think I've learned enough about the RV lifestyle that will be of use to others. At least, that is my intent.

Many of the topics I have written about pertain to the full-timing lifestyle; many others relate to motorhoming. All, however, have some relevance to a lifestyle that is unique and exciting, whether it is pursued for days, or months, or years. I'm sure that many readers will empathize with some of our experiences, and hopefully, learn from some of them.

Happy travelin'!

■ ■ ■

Changing Places

I met a fellow the other day who told me that when he started full-timing many years ago, he threw away his watch and his maps. When people ask him what time it is, he answers, "Now." When they ask where he is going, he responds, "Here." Although his comments are made rather facetiously, they reflect an attitude that is very common with one type of fulltimer. At the other extreme, there are some people who are almost completely "programmed," that is, their life plan is strictly scheduled and routed.

Fulltiming is a very democratic lifestyle. It accommodates all kinds of interpretations—where to go, how to go, what to do. Many life-on-the-road practitioners try a bit of everything at one time or another. Some, however, opt for a path from which they seldom deviate.

As a kind of review, a jogging of the memory, it might be wise for each of us occasionally to take a look at some of the alternatives to our usual way of doing our thing.

For example, how long has it been since you boondocked? Or have you ever? Of course, in some parts of the country, there are few interesting places for that approach to RV living. Most of the government lands open to boondockers are in the West, primarily in Arizona, California, Utah, and Nevada.

An exceptionally popular place with RVers is Quartzsite, Arizona, which has enough space for an almost unlimited number of recreational vehicles, interesting things for RVers to do and relatively close-by necessities to maintain the lifestyle (water, dump facilities, propane, groceries —even a McDonald's not too far down the highway!).

But if you prefer a more primitive ambience, there are plenty of places quite remote from any of the common signs of human progress in the western deserts. The Bureau of Land Management offices will gladly provide information upon request.

Some fulltimers start out with specific destinations, i.e., every state or every national park and monument. They may designate a route and set a calendar. Their progress follows the itinerary they set for themselves. The folks who follow these plans derive satisfaction and comfort in meeting their schedules. And, upon completion of one major program, they create another.

Another popular approach to fulltiming is avid participation in club activities. Many staunch members can be seen at every major rally, often helping out in some way.

Fulltimers who have hobbies or vocations that involve products or services they sell may follow a circuit, visiting various kinds of shows, arts and crafts fairs, and flea markets. Their travels are directed generally by the destinations at which they can do business.

Snowbirds may be types that move only twice a year—once to their chosen southern winter roost and again in the spring to a place in the north. Some rent or lease spaces on a seasonal basis, and others even buy their own. Many snowbirds have those basic summer and winter places, but they include a few stops in between. Other snowbirds don't settle very long in specific spots but move up and down the country with the seasons, enjoying a variety of people, places, and things.

Fulltimers have an almost infinite variety of choices in how they can do their thing. We probably should all take stock now and then of how we do our thing, and, just for kicks, change our pace. Maybe we even can throw away our watches and maps for a while!

■ ■ ■

July 1991

Lucky Us

Americans are blessed with varied and wonderful opportunities to travel and see the world. But we are particularly fortunate in being able to see some of the best without leaving the boundaries of the United States, one of the greatest vacation countries in the world.

Mother Nature has been especially kind with a generous endowment of varied terrain: thousands of miles of seacoasts, numerous mountain ranges, acres of desert landscape, and everything else imaginable.

The breakers pound fearsomely and chillingly on the rugged coasts of Maine and Oregon; the sandy beaches and warm surf of the Carolinas and California lure millions of people, both young and old, in midsummer; the tepid waters of the Gulf of Mexico make the coasts of Florida and Texas particularly attractive to older snowbirds. Whether you want swimming, surfing, sunbathing, fishing, or just admiring, the United States has every conceivable type of beach—and an abundance of them.

When it comes to mountains, we really lucked out. There are the aged, weathered-down Appalachians; the endless, hazy hills of the Smokies; and the rugged, saw-toothed peaks of the Rockies and the Sierra Nevada. Other ranges give evidence of our past and present geological transformations. The Earth's crust in the United States offers observers a fascinating story. Those who have stood at Artist's Point in Yellowstone, or driven the Going-to-the-Sun Mountain road in Glacier National Park, or stood at Lookout Mountain in Tennessee, or viewed the devastation wrought by Mount St. Helens in Washington know what I mean.

Certainly not the least of our topographical marvels are the seem-
ingly endless deserts in the West. From the outskirts of San Antonio
to the suburbs of Los Angeles, from the upper reaches of Utah to the
Mexican border, nature's parsimony with moisture has created millions
of acres of dry, sparsely vegetated but incredibly beautiful deserts.

Have you have ever seen Arizona's Painted Desert, the pink spires
of Utah's Bryce Canyon, the saguaro forests of Arizona, the vast, still
plains of Death Valley, or the fiery blooms at the ends of ocotillo wands
in California's Anza-Borrego Desert? If so, you can appreciate the desert
country's arid beauty.

When it comes to man-made attractions, let's face it: The "book" was
written here. We have the great Disney attractions, Sea Worlds galore,
and Silver Dollar City in Branson, Missouri; the list is endless. And who
can count the number of incredible shopping attractions! There's Union
Station in St. Louis; Vanity Fair in Harrisburg, Pennsylvania; and the
outlet malls in Pigeon Forge, Tennessee—just to name a few.

Then there are our innumerable historical places: battlefields, old
mining towns, famous people's homes and famous-event monuments,
all commemorating significant steps in our country's history. You can't
tour the battlefield at Gettysburg without experiencing some feeling for
the soldiers who struggled there; you can't visit Fort McHenry without
a deeper appreciation for "The Star Spangled Banner;" and you can't
tour the old mining town of Cripple Creek, Colorado, without gaining
some understanding of a miner's life.

Indeed, we are fortunate to be able to visit our past, enjoy man-made
attractions in our present, and experience the beauty of our country's
natural surroundings at any time. And there's no better way to discover
our history and our future than to travel the country by motorhome!

■ ■ ■

August 1991

Let's Go Camping

otorhomers need to take a real camping trip every now and then to be reminded of the original purpose of RVs. Many of us have strayed so far from our first RVing experience that we have almost forgotten the simple pleasure of watching the dancing flames of a campfire . . . hearing the shouts of children reveling amid one of Mother Nature's many pleasures . . . smelling the tantalizing aromas wafting from campsite barbecues at dusk. Nowadays, these sights, sounds, and scents aren't much a part of the adult RV resorts in the Sun Belt.

In the beginning, homes on wheels were intended to enable outdoor lovers to enjoy their outings with a greater degree of comfort than offered by tents and sleeping bags. However, the change from the relatively simple trailers and motorized rigs of the fifties and sixties to the luxurious RVs of today has been paralleled by the development of places to use those marvelous machines. And, in the process, many of us have neglected the chief reason that we took up RVing in the first place.

Like most of today's motorhomers, Margie and I started out as conventional campers back in the early fifties. We packed up the tent, sleeping bags, a stove, lanterns, and boxes of miscellaneous gear, and headed for the campgrounds where the only amenities were water spigots and outhouses. But, best of all, there was a lot of beautiful nature— trees, mountains, beaches, deserts. We fished, hiked, swam, loafed, read, and ate.

The kids grew up, left home, and then it all changed. Somehow, our outings became different—no more tents or tent trailers, and soon no more camping. As our time away from home increased, so did our desire for the comforts of home. The result was bigger motorhomes with more bells and whistles, and luxury RV parks with more amenities.

I would be the first to admit that I don't want to go back to a tent and a sleeping bag, but a recent week's stay at an oceanfront state park was an excellent reminder that we still do enjoy camping. Of course, camping in a motorhome isn't roughing it, but roughing it doesn't head my list of things to do. However, a whole week without hookups and television was something that we hadn't experienced in a long time. Yes, we missed those amenities, but their absence was more than compensated for by those special camping experiences that are absent in the parks we generally visit.

We especially enjoyed the kids. One of the mixed blessings of snowbird parks is that they are usually "adults only." On the one hand, it's nice not to be in a kid-dominated atmosphere—no loud radios, no bicycles hurtling in every direction, no bathroom disaster areas, and no screaming kids being yelled at by harried parents. On the other hand, as grandparents of six, we sometimes get homesick for kids—noises, messes, and all. We were reminded of that real world as we watched the water-balloon fights, the sand forts being built, the teenage boys bashfully trying to make points with the girls, and, perhaps best of all, the beautiful babies.

This camping outing has been a great reminder for us that even adventurous motorhomers can get in a rut. That rut can become the easy way and not necessarily the most fun way. I don't think that we are about to take up a life of roughing it, but I suspect that we will start looking at our maps a little more carefully for public parks that have campgrounds.

Try camping some time!

■ ■ ■

October 1991

Setting New Goals

Theoretically, the retirement years are a time when the big "have-to" goals in life—such as making a living, raising a family, buying a home and establishing financial security—have been realized. For full- or extended-time RVers who are retired, it can be a time for setting new goals. Only now, goal setting can be made on a "want-to" rather than a "have-to" basis.

For some RVers, fulltiming means making no plans other than to take each day and place as it comes. Most of us, however, relish some feelings of achievement—and in order to accomplish something, we must have goals.

Many RVers can remember when vacations were too brief because of limited time permitted away from work, when trips were too short because finances were skimpy, and when destinations were limited because of the need to choose places that were family-oriented. Now, with more time and money—and no kids—those constraints have been lifted.

Probably one of the most frequent entries on travel wish lists is the desire to visit all fifty states—or, at least, all forty-eight contiguous ones. Of course, not everyone immediately sets out to attain this goal, but the idea seems to always be there. Although it wasn't earthshaking, I remember well the feeling of accomplishment when we finally covered the last of the forty-eight states. (Vermont and New Hampshire had eluded us until just about five years ago!)

Some people are satisfied with just traveling to every state, but most RVers who have an all-states goal also pursue some specific objectives while touring each one. Sometimes it is exploring the state capitals and taking tours of the capitol buildings, or visiting the various special state attractions. Many RVers enjoy the unique scenic beauty and natural wonders of some states, and seek out national parks, forests, or monuments. Others delight in spectacular man-made attractions, such as Disney World, Silver Dollar City, and Bourbon Street. Historical points of interest and locations also provide interesting destinations.

An interesting goal that one RVing couple established was to visit every relative. Armed with the family genealogy and a well-prepared address book, they mapped out a journey that took them through many states. On a trip that extended from coast to coast, they planned to enjoy reunions with dozens of vaguely remembered cousins, aunts, and uncles, as well as expecting to see many other memorable places.

RVers set all kinds of special-interest destinations, including stops at major museums, golf courses, big shopping centers, important auto racetracks, and baseball games at every major league stadium. Several couples I've met even have targeted the unique or ethnic cuisines associated with different regions of the country.

Reader's Digest and *National Geographic* magazines have published excellent guides to travel destinations in the United States. You can find areas of interest, indicated in red or green, in Rand McNally atlases.

The review could continue indefinitely, but surely the point is clear: Many RVers enjoy traveling with some sort of goal or plan to fulfill. So, set some new goals—and decide on your destination.

■ ■ ■

November 1991

Boondocking

Just mention boondocking in a group of RVers and you'll get very definite and very different reactions. Some love it; some hate it. Others are fascinated by the idea, and like a cold lake, they dip their toes in now and then but never take the plunge. But hardly anyone is without an opinion on the subject.

For the benefit of the novice, boondocking means literally setting up camp in the boondocks—deserted, isolated areas without facilities, usually BLM (Bureau of Land Management) lands. Generally, that means there are some popular spots in a few states. The larger boondock camps are relatively close (within twenty-five miles) to basic shopping facilities. The best known are the Slabs (near Niland, California); the Imperial Dam area, including Senator Wash (near Yuma, Arizona); Pilot Knob (in California just west of Yuma); and Quartzsite, Arizona. There are scores of less-well-known boondocking locations frequented by just a few rigs or the loner who wants total privacy.

Although Margie and I are only toe-dippers when it comes to boondocking (Quartzsite a couple of times, and two or three stops at Senator Wash), I've been quietly studying boondockers for years. I'm trying to find out just what makes them tick. So far, I've concluded that their requirements are about as varied as those of motorhomers who stay only in urban RV resorts. You just can't list them all under the same heading.

Some motorhomers boondock for economic reasons. Except for the $25 season fee that the BLM imposes for those who stay more than two weeks in one place, there are no charges. So for those with a very limited income, the price is right. However, since most large boondock camps are in the general area of simple RV parks that offer full hookups for under $100 a month, the economic reason may be secondary.

Most boondockers simply prefer that lifestyle. They like the simplicity of everyday living, the privacy, the closeness with nature, and the adventure of being back to basics in meeting life's challenges.

Some boondockers like the challenges of primitive living conditions, but they pay for that preference in extra chores, such as bringing in fresh water and emptying the holding tank.

The BLM's efforts to provide fresh water and dump stations at major boondock camps (with the $25 user fees) has helped, but only by cutting the distance that it must be carried. Keeping electrical systems powered is one of the biggest challenges. Fortunately, RVers are generally innovative, and, with the assortment of gadgets currently available, they solve their power problems, which a lot of men enjoy doing.

Since most boondockers are quite distant from towns, shopping is, for most, quite an inconvenience. Not only is the problem of distance involved, but the kind of roads one must traverse can make travel slow and uncomfortable. Anyone who has driven a dozen miles of the unimproved, dusty, bumpy, twisting desert road back of Senator Wash knows what I mean. For obvious reasons, boondockers keep going to town at a minimum.

I talk to many RVers who say they would like to try boondocking but don't know where to begin. I always advise them to make that first try at Quartzsite around Pow-Wow time (end of January/first of February). I assure you that boondocking at Quartzsite isn't a retreat from civilization, but it is an excellent place to really learn what self-containment is all about.

■ ■ ■

January 1992

Motorhome Guests

I nviting guests to travel with you can be a delightful way to take a special motorhome trip—especially if it is someone you're very close to, such as your parents or grandchildren. On the other hand, guests can spell disaster. A motorhome's very limited floor space mandates harmony. When extra roomers turn out to be lemons, everyone gets the puckers.

Margie and I have taken guests with us on many occasions, but we've been fortunate in never having a serious guest problem. I was reminded, however, of the potential for disaster by the experience of an RV friend who told me that he had recently returned from a week of hell. Inviting a couple with whom he and his wife had been bosom buddies for many years was an excellent idea, but taking their twelve-year-old daughter wasn't. The bosom buddies had a great time for the first couple of days, and then the bored preteen decided to make everyone as miserable as she was. It was then that our friends discovered the real meaning of the word *brat*. The part of the trip they enjoyed most was the end of it.

There are no sure-fire rules for choosing motorhome guests, but common sense works most of the time. Common sense tells me that anyone I'm going to share a few hundred square feet with for twenty-four hours a day should be someone I like a whole bunch—a person I can get peeved at, but still love.

Once you deviate from a policy of "family members only," you set the stage for disaster. You can know people for a long time and believe that you really know them, but nothing will reveal their real selves like living with them in a confined space. As I always tell people in my seminar on fulltiming, "There ain't much fightin' room in an RV."

One of the major problems with taking guests is that, in spite of the fact that most manufacturers claim their rigs will sleep six or sleep eight, few rigs actually sleep more than two people comfortably. Consequently, someone—or some people—end up sleeping on less-than-comfortable beds.

Booths or tables that "seat four" don't always do so comfortably either. In fact, compared with the comforts and space that people are accustomed to in houses, some motorhomes are downright uncomfortable when more than two people try to live in them.

If you decide to take guests RVing, establish some criteria for choosing them. There are some general guidelines that will help you avoid the pitfall that befell my friend. Try answering these questions first:

1. Do you really want anyone with you? Guests can alter your established routines, sometimes forcing changes that you don't want.

2. What are the characteristics about your potential guests that you would find difficult to tolerate? Few people have relatives or friends who are perfect, so you know that you will have to tolerate their imperfections if you decide to take these people with you.

3. Do the guests generally like what you like in terms of travel? Obviously, if you like to dawdle everywhere, there will definitely be a conflict with guests who like to live on the fast track. If your idea of a good trip is visiting historical places and natural wonders, you may end up being at odds with people who favor shopping malls and Disneyland.

4. Can you disagree with your guests and still remain buddies? Most people can usually survive family squabbles without serious consequences. But other folks cannot resolve their differences, and that can mark the beginning of the end of a friendship.

5. Do your guests have children? If so, can you tolerate them? If the answer is no, you had better think twice about inviting them.

■ ■ ■

February 1992

Those Precious Things!

Pack rats are noted for their tendency to accumulate things. Discoverers of their treasure troves are amazed at the diligence and ingenuity reflected in the quantity and diversity of their handiwork.

But the efforts of pack rats pale in comparison with the accumulative spirit of Homo sapiens. Blessed or cursed with a never-ending offering of things, humans are addicted to the quest for acquiring at least one each of everything manufactured by man or nature. And, unfortunately, the effects of that addiction are compounded by an equally strong reluctance to ever throw away anything.

I don't mean to suggest that everything we own is worthless and should be tossed out. It's just that so much of it is superfluous; it's unused, not usable, and of no real value—things such as broken tools that all men seem to treasure. Why is it that we keep shovels with broken handles? Oh, I know. We think that some day we are going to replace the handles, but we never do. Why do men who wear size 40 (or larger) pants still keep pants that are long outgrown in their closets? Do they really think that some day they'll again fit those smaller sizes?

Women are equally guilty of the same kind of trash collecting. They keep broken picture frames, chipped cups they will never use, purses they never carry, and used Christmas wrapping paper that will never embellish another gift.

Generally the fact is that we load ourselves up with a lot of material stuff that we don't really use, need, or care about. Most of us could, without a sense of loss, divest ourselves of all but the basic things that we actually use, such as clothes that we wear, tools that work, and the essential pots, pans, dishes, etc. It's a tough decision, but it's one that all fulltimers have to make when they take to the road. Therein lies a dilemma.

I've heard of all kinds of solutions. Some are the obvious, such as yard sales, auctions, or estate sales. Others are more imaginative and better in the long run. My favorite is one used by many couples who are ready to shed the irrelevant material things as they prepare for life on wheels. Simply, it is to offer all those extra things to the children. Let the kids pick and choose from the furniture they grew up with, the tools they learned to use under Dad's gentle tutelage or stern orders, and the doodads and knickknacks on tables, shelves, and walls (some of which they collected as kids).

The nice thing about giving your stuff to the kids is that you will still be able to visit it later, if you so choose. Remember, Dad, that your chair won't be yours anymore. It will be your son's chair, and he will probably order you out of it—just as you did to him!

A method of distributing your things fairly among several kids is this: Give each an equal amount of Monopoly or other play money, and conduct an auction. That way, the kids will establish priorities and values on individual items, and each should end up with approximately an equal share of the family's treasures. You'll be surprised by what they don't want. Give the leftovers to your grandchildren, neighbors, or a charitable organization. In the latter case, you should request a receipt for your probably enormous contribution, which will be of some value at tax time.

For those who find it difficult to part with superfluous possessions, perhaps it will ease your mind to know that of all the hundreds of fulltimers I have interviewed, I have never found one who grieved for the loss of his or her "precious things."

■ ■ ■

April 1992

French Boudoirs

T here's nothing wrong with motorhomes looking nice, but do they have to look like French boudoirs? Especially those models with elaborate fixtures, exquisite upholstery fabrics, rare-wood cabinets and paneling, and other features that are reminiscent of Leona Helmsley's hotels.

Don't get me wrong. I'm not advocating that motorhomes should be dull and drab. My concern is that an overfocus on bells and whistles and plushness may have contributed to motorhome prices going off the chart. And, from a purely practical standpoint, some motorhomes are so elegant that I'd almost be afraid to use them because I might get them dirty.

I suspect that some readers may be wondering if I've changed my personal feelings about all the great gadgets and goodies available for motorhomes. I assure you I haven't. However, I would like to make a distinction between the limits of what is practical and what is impractical.

Perhaps there's a thin line separating those two things, a line that varies according to the interpreter. Although we may disagree somewhat on where that line is, I suspect most of us would agree that, in our eagerness and willingness to accept the grandiosity that manufacturers offer us, we sometimes forego practicality for glitz.

Unfortunately, many of us find ourselves trying to keep up with the Joneses. Someone in the club gets a Super Wonderhome and the first thing you know, everyone starts trading up. Those fabulous gadgets and plush furnishings can be irresistible temptations. I can't help but wonder how many proud new owners of those elegant wheeled palaces quickly find themselves changing their entire approach to motorhoming. Instead of directing their activities toward camping (nature, fishing, backroads, boondocking, campgrounds), they are almost forced into resorting (golfing, loafing in elegant surroundings, partying, dancing, RV resorts).

As one who has been a part of the RV industry since the late 1950s and has witnessed the development of the motorhome since its infancy, I have seen dramatic changes during that thirty-year period. From a design standpoint, the most dramatic change has been an evolution from motorhomes that were primarily a superior means of camping to motorhomes that are wheeled palaces.

I'm not blaming anyone for this evolutionary process of luxury in motorhome manufacturing. Certainly, manufacturers wouldn't emphasize glitz if buyers weren't receptive to the idea. One major manufacturer remarked to me, "Whatever the public wants, we'll build."

We consumers are a fickle bunch. We say we want simple, economical motorhomes, but then turn right around and compare them with elegant, plush, costly models. That makes it tough for a manufacturer who has to try to figure out what consumers really want most and are actually willing to buy.

Recently, I had the opportunity to be on both sides of the fence as both the designer of a motorhome and the consumer. I am referring to the "perfect full-timer's rig" project I've been involved with for more than a year. In the thousands of suggestions I received from readers, I can honestly say that there were very few references to aesthetics. In designing the perfect rig, I spent very little time considering glitzy features. Function and practicality were primary concerns.

Now that I'm road-testing and living in the prototype, I'm content to leave French boudoirs in France.

■ ■ ■

May 1992

Say Howdy

L et's compare two scenarios. First scenario: You're walking down the sidewalk in a big city. Someone approaches you from the opposite direction. The odds are you will ignore the other person, probably by looking in another direction or down at your feet, and you won't speak.

Second scenario: You are walking through an RV park, and you see a stranger coming toward you. What is your reaction? The odds are you'll look the person in the eye, smile and say "howdy" or some other such greeting.

So, what's the point? I believe it's this: The RV lifestyle is conducive to good-neighborliness. RVers are more inclined to take the first step toward knowing the people around them. Not only are they willing to talk to each other, but they are also usually willing to lend a hand when it is needed. In short, there's obviously something about living in a motorhome that makes people look on the bright side of life, especially when it comes to their relationships with other people.

Why this is true, I'm not sure. It could be that the lifestyle creates friendly people or, possibly, the reverse—that friendly people create the lifestyle. Quite likely, it is a combination of the two. But whatever the reason, I don't think many observers would disagree with my claim that we RVers live together more like friendly, country neighbors than typical, detached big-city residents who don't want to be involved with those living around them.

Lest someone charge that I have a tendency to idealize RVers, to see only the good side about them while ignoring those who don't fit my stereotype, let me assure you that I have met some RV-turkeys in the three decades that I have been an RVer. Recently, in fact, while Margie and I were walking in the campground where we stopped for the night, we noted gobs of transmission-fluid-stained paper towels that had been wadded up and thrown on the ground at a just-vacated space. I didn't see the person who did it, but I assume he wouldn't be the friendly, good-neighbor type! Unfortunately, I spotted that messed-up space and ignored the dozens that were left clean and neat. I try to accept the fact that there will always be aberrations—even among RVers.

Actually, I attribute the creation of the friendly RVer stereotype to several factors. RVers are more likely to be older folks (or should I say, more mature), many of whom are probably retirees. I can't help but conclude that there's something about advancing years that loosens up people. Perhaps it's the fact that they are no longer competing for money, power, or the opposite sex the way younger people do.

In analyzing the RV lifestyle, I've come to the conclusion that the feeling of security that comes with living in RV resorts and campgrounds goes a long way toward promoting camaraderie among the participants. Anyone who has lived or presently lives in a town of any size knows what I mean. The threat to individuals and property is at an all-time high in most places. Many city people are distrustful of each other—and with good reason.

But crime isn't everywhere. Generally, it is conspicuously absent in RV resorts and campgrounds. Of course, there are occasional reports of thefts from RVs or campsites, but they are rare. As for violence against other people, it is almost unheard of among RVers. As I have often said, the bad guys don't go for RVing.

Nope. RVers have a pleasant "howdy" for each other.

■ ■ ■

June 1992

Dumb Stunts

S how me a motorhome owner who doesn't occasionally do some kind of dumb stunt, and I'll show you a motorhomer who does not use his motorhome. The fact is that combining a house with a truck and having people live on wheels is a sure recipe for catastrophes, mostly minor, but sometimes real whoppers.

I've had my share of them—like the time I rushed off one rainy morning, with the motorhome's power cord looped around a power pole. The bump I felt and heard was a relatively minor one, but the damage I did to the electrical box on the motorhome was definitely major; the repair bill was significant.

Here are some other doozies. I'm sure that most motorhome owners regularly flush their holding tanks and, after draining them completely, fill and flush them out. I'm still chagrined about the time a few years ago when I was performing this chore at a campground. With the toilet pedal blocked open to fill the black-water tank, I had a memory lapse about what I was doing and took a walk. As you might surmise, the tank filled and the entire motorhome started to fill. When a neighbor saw water running out from the rig's floor, he shut off the spigot. As you might suspect, I had quite a drying-out job to do.

I've done a lot of these minor dumb stunts that don't really cause any serious damage. Mostly, they are embarrassing and aggravating—like the time a fellow in the back seat of the car in front of me looked back and started making various gesticulations, including pointing upward. I misinterpreted his sign as a variation of "the bird" and returned his salute. Finally, I realized that he was indicating our antenna was up. Even though I backed off quickly, I'm sure that he glimpsed my scarlet face.

Back in the old days when refrigerator doors had to be secured with pins while traveling, I forgot to take care of that chore on several occasions. I recall my first big lesson, which occurred when I turned a corner just a few blocks from home in our first brand-new motorhome. Our well-stocked refrigerator completely emptied on the brand-new carpeting. It was awhile before we forgot to put the pin in the door again.

Then there was the time I tried to take off with my leveling jacks fully extended. Fortunately, the rear wheels were off the ground enough that it didn't do anything—except to my ego.

Of a more serious nature was my dumb decision to go down a long 13 percent grade with a car hooked on and pushing from behind. When the brakes overheated, I almost didn't stop midway.

Yep, I've done some doozies, but a good friend of mine topped all of my dumb stunts put together with a single performance. Last fall, this very learned fellow (a retired nuclear engineer) got a few miles down the road from home when he realized that something wasn't right. When he stopped and examined his tow car, he discovered the ultimate super-whopper dumb stunt: His car's transmission was in reverse. Needless to say, he is very careful with his new car, and his misfortune is making me even more careful about my motorhoming.

I'm pretty well convinced that many of us need to make a checklist before we take off, just like airplane pilots. I find that particularly true with every new rig that I buy, especially as I get older. So I've devised a new list to follow (see page 24), which Margie and I faithfully adhere to before I fire up our new diesel—except when we forget!

■ ■ ■

September 1992

Dining Out Versus Eating Out

The downfall of many an RVer in both paunch and purse stems from those fateful words: "Let's eat out tonight." We make all kinds of excuses for ducking the cooking chores: "It's just as cheap to eat out as it is to cook;" or, "I can fix dinner but it will take an hour;" or, "We could run over to that little restaurant across the street and grab a bite right now."

Restaurants are routine winners of those rationalizations for evading ordinary culinary chores. That's why there are so many of them in areas frequented by large numbers of RVers.

However, most visits to restaurants mean rounds lost in the calorie fight and additional dents in the budget. In the nutrition department, I have little practical advice to offer. The constant bombardment we get from the media is more than sufficient to make experts of us all. In fact, we all know what's good for us, and we either do the right thing or we don't. But when it comes to financial advice on eating out, I have some pearls of wisdom.

It is important to understand the difference between dining out and eating out. Experts don't agree on what these phrases mean. For example, some would assert that any restaurant that uses tablecloths is a dining place. Others say both tablecloth and cloth napkins are necessary for that categorization. Still others claim that it takes both of those plus two forks to be a true dining establishment.

I am not aware of any absolute rule for distinguishing true dining, but I can give you a perfect example of real dining out. A couple of years ago we visited Chalet Suzanne in Lake Wales, Florida. It is an absolutely wonderful place, loaded with charm, friendliness, and impeccable service. Menus evoke the same type of sticker shock as MSRP stickers on new Cadillacs. Even the lowly barnyard fowl achieves elevated status, with Chicken Suzanne going for $49.50! You can imagine what the expensive items like steak and seafood cost. A couple celebrating an anniversary that includes a pre-dinner nip, a plate of appetizers, and a bottle of wine with the meal would very likely see a tab of around $200. (However, some good news: According to a notation on the menu, tipping is not necessary. The bad news: An 18 percent service charge is added to each bill!)

I may not be positively clear about the distinction between eating out and dining out, but I do know that anyone who has a meal at Chalet Suzanne very definitely dines out.

On the other hand, that same couple might consider an alternative and celebrate their anniversary by simply eating out, like at Denny's. On the senior menu, you can get a five-course dinner for $3.59. You pay with a ten-spot and still get enough change to meet the price of a full bottle of Ripple for an after-dinner binge back at the motorhome. Now that's eating out.

My point is that many motorhomers, especially fulltimers, are prone to take the quick and easy way at mealtime. Eating out—specifically, dining out—can warp a budget quicker than anything I know. The careful budget-watcher should be very conscious of the financial implications of eating out and dining out when opting for the alternative to cooking in.

If you are serious about a budget, allocate a food fund at the beginning of the month, and pay for all your food from that fund. A dine-out or two during the month will prove my point.

So, the next time your spouse suggests eating out, be sure to ask if she or he really means eating—or dining.

■ ■ ■

October 1992

Pre-Flight Check

A irplanes don't crash very often. One of the chief reasons they tend to stay in the air is that pilots always do a pre-flight check. They try to make sure that their airplanes are as ready to fly as they can be before they take off. Smart motorhomers do the same thing before they hit the road.

I suppose there are motorhomers who have never driven off with something not properly prepared, but I've never met them. Most of us have good intentions. We try to remember to check everything before we fire up, but we sometimes forget or overlook things. The results range all the way from exasperating to catastrophic. How many times we have pulled out of a park onto a highway shortly to find that a roof vent had been left open, or, worse yet, arriving somewhere on a dirt or gravel road and discovering an inch of dust in the bedroom from a half-open window. Exasperating! Of course, catastrophes occur when such things as oil and coolant are neglected. After each bad experience, we vow to be more careful in the future.

I've found that the only sure way to be certain that everything is ready before driving off is to use a checklist just like airplane pilots. The few minutes that it takes each time to do the checkoff can prevent numerous hours and dollars from being spent in cleanup and repairs.

Over the years we've devised a number of motorhome pre-flight checklists. Although there has been some variation due to different rigs with different features, the basics remain the same. For example we now have a diesel engine, and it is very important that there be a warm-up period before taking off and a cooldown period before shutting down.

As is the case in so many situations, good intentions are often ignored or overlooked for various reasons. Haste is the major malefactor for me. In a hurry to get going, I am inclined to jump behind the wheel, fire up, and hurtle off. Margie has cured me somewhat of that tendency, though. With the list taped to the front of our atlas, which is always on the dash, she grabs it just as I start the engine and in no uncertain terms insists that we do our checkoff. Then, while the engine warms up, she reads off the items, and I verify that things are ready for takeoff. (Incidentally for those of you who think you have a foolproof method of getting ready without a list, double-check yourself a few times and see how often you overlook something.) Of course, everyone who makes a checklist tailors it to his or her particular way of doing things. That's great. But for those who haven't devised a list on their own, I'd be happy to share ours. It can be added to as one desires:

■ ■ ■

November 1992

Rude Awakening

Talk about rude awakenings! At 4:58 A.M. on June 28, we really had one when a major earthquake hit Southern California as we were sleeping in an upstairs bedroom at my sister's house in San Dimas. The house shuddered; loose objects rattled and fell; the noise was thunderous. We were roughly ejected from our bed.

As earthquake veterans, we knew immediately what was happening. Having experienced quite a number of quakes without suffering property damage or personal injury during the three decades that we lived in that area, we were not terrified out of our wits. However, to say that we were uncomfortable would be putting it mildly We would much rather have been somewhere else at the time. In fact, a thought that popped into my mind was: I wish we were in our motorhome.

You see, I believe that being in a motorhome is, in most cases, the safest place you can be when natural disasters strike—particularly earthquakes. Television and newspaper reports make us aware of the tremendous damages, injuries, and sometimes even deaths that often accompany major earthquakes. Scenes of demolished buildings, collapsed bridges, the removal of bodies, and stories of people being buried alive for days follow every major quake. But did you ever see a picture or read a report of similar disaster involving people in motorhomes?

Margie and I have been in our motorhome during several earthquakes. Although we felt some vibration, it was much less severe than you usually feel in a building, and there were no falling objects. The fact that a motorhome is designed to be driven, to be twisted and turned, and to take the bumps of less-than-perfect roads makes earthquake tremors small stuff indeed.

It is not uncommon for people to prepare refuges for times of disaster. People in many areas of the country have storm cellars to retreat to when violent storms threaten. Bomb shelters were popular in the late 1950s and 1960s when there was a real threat of nuclear war, and ships carry provisioned lifeboats. History proves that people who prepare in advance for disasters usually suffer the least when they strike.

I'm firmly convinced that the best way to prepare for the Big One that is theoretically imminent in California is to live in a motorhome—or at least have a well-provisioned motorhome available for use as an emergency shelter in case a disastrous quake occurs. If you are in the motorhome when the tremors hit, you are in a much safer place than in a building, so the chances of injury from a collapsing house or falling objects are practically nil. With a good supply of canned goods on hand; full water, propane, and gasoline tanks; and fully charged batteries, you may choose to leave a disaster area promptly if road conditions permit, or stay in the devastated area with a fully operational home.

My advice to motorhomers in earthquake areas is to think of the coach as a lifeboat. Prepare it for the emergency that you hope will never happen. If it does, you will be in a much better position to cope with circumstances that might otherwise be insurmountable.

Keep the motorhome ready for immediate use. Decide what you would need for survival in a worst-case scenario and prepare now. When the Big One hits—when the buildings crack and fall; when the water, gas, and electricity go off; when fires rage and terror reigns—is not the time to begin your emergency preparations.

After all, there's nothing better than being ready to roll at any time, for any reason.

■ ■ ■

December 1992

Copiloting

There's nothing like a good copilot to simplify the work of the motorhome driver and enhance the motorhoming experience. On the other hand, a bad copilot can un-make a motorhome driver's day like you can't believe. Wise travelers clearly understand and follow through with their individual roles in the driving process.

I've broken what I consider a good copilot's duties to be into three categories: navigation, providing information, and gofering. Of the three, navigational assistance is by far the most important to me.

Although I always check a map before taking off, I can only remember just so many details. Unfortunately, I have a habit of forgetting crucial information at critical times—like when we reach a fork in the road and I've forgotten which route to take. And when driving through the middle of a city and suddenly approaching an intersection with sixteen branches of the freeway going in every direction, it's difficult to make a split decision on which one to take. The observant copilot, who at those times comes up with life-saving information like "Take the next exit," or "Follow I-5 right through town," indeed earns his or her keep.

I recommend that the copilot always keep the map open. You should know exactly where you are at all times. That doesn't mean constantly looking at the map, but it does mean always being aware of where you are and being able to find your location on the map. Also, the good copilot always knows what special points are ahead, including rest stops, mountain passes, towns, parks, and places of interest. A five-minute study of the day's projected route before takeoff and an hourly orientation on where you are are usually sufficient to keep the pilot well informed and the copilot prepared to provide information quickly.

Good copilots can provide information only as good as the sources of information they use. Those who travel extensively should have an excellent supply of maps. A current road atlas is a necessity, as it will have the latest information on road changes. Besides an atlas, I also like to carry maps of metropolitan areas where we will be visiting various places and people. We find historical maps particularly useful, too; those that are published by the National Geographic Society are the best available.

The second chore category for the copilot is providing miscellaneous useful information. For example, we start out a day's driving with a brief map study and the selection of a probable destination for that day. When it becomes clear where we will be spending the night, my copilot, Margie, uses the current *Trailer Life Directory* to locate a specific park. She reads the information to me as we travel, and together we decide on a stopping point. Sometimes Margie studies brochures or other sources of information about places we expect to visit and shares the information with me as we cruise along.

Besides the information we glean from brochures and booklets about various places in the United States, we carry with us some special books about Civil War battlefields and other historical or natural points of interest.

Finally, every pilot needs a gofer. Margie is great at that job. She'll gofer a coke; she'll gofer a snack at lunchtime, she'll gofer a certain book or magazine when I need specific information. Her assistance makes it possible for us to keep rolling while I enjoy the creature comforts others might have to stop for.

Blessed is the motorhome driver who has a good copilot.

■ ■ ■

January 1993

Setting a Pace

One of the biggest complaints we hear from people nowadays is that everyday living demands such a frantic pace. City people, particularly, seem hell-bent to reach some place or something from early morning until late at night. Apparently, they have no control over that big rush. They can't slow down—even if they want to—because they feel caught in something bigger than themselves.

Full-time RVers, on the other hand, set their own pace. Whether fast or slow, it's up to the individuals how quickly they get somewhere or do something.

Pace is determined by planning. For example, some RVers like to see as many things as possible as quickly as possible. Even as full-time RVers, they move about a great deal and are constantly nudged by a need to keep moving.

At the other extreme are those fulltimers who turtle-crawl their way around the country—moving slowly and infrequently. The word "hurry" is not in their vocabulary. Generally, they don't wear watches.

Most of us fit somewhere in between. Although it isn't uncommon for most of us to hurry at times, usually our pace is moderate. But there is one thing common to all fulltimers: We set our own life's speed-control.

Pace is determined a great deal by interests. Lovers of the backroads, nature, small towns, and minor attractions are more apt to be less rushed than those who stick to the interstates, cities, and grand, man-made attractions. The former type might very well get up when he feels like it, choose a scenic highway that wends its way along a river, stop at U.S. Forest Service campgrounds, and read all historic signs along the road. Hours or even days are spent seeing and enjoying. The pace is s-l-o-o-o-w.

Conversely, the latter type of RVer barrels down the interstates between big cities where he or she spends much of the time zipping from one tourist trap to another. This type spends minutes—hours at most—seeing the things the slow-pacers dawdle over for days or weeks.

Although these two approaches vary greatly, neither is right nor wrong. The slow-paced folks like to savor their objectives. When visiting a museum, they plan to see everything, to linger at exhibits. The fast-paced travelers frequently schedule lots of places and things to do. Their attitude is that there is so much to see that they have to limit their time at each in order to cover as much ground as possible. Their "idle" is always running.

Personally, I feel that the turtles are on the right track. But some folks, especially those who retired from a lifetime of rushing, find it difficult to slow down. So, if you are one of those who feels the need to cover at least 500 miles a day while stopping at a half-dozen tourist attractions, always hit campgrounds after dark, eat at fast-food restaurants most of the time, look at your watch every fifteen minutes, and get impatient if your spouse wants to read all the tombstones at old cemeteries, perhaps you need to take a few lessons in pace adjustment.

First, plan your travels and stops at places and things that interest you. Just because a place is designated an attraction isn't a guarantee that you will like it. On the other hand, I urge you to try things that aren't familiar. Many fulltimers discover new interests as they travel.

Second, limit the number of things you try to see and the amount of miles you travel. See things more fully when you do stop.

Third, carefully plan your travel itinerary, including definite places and things you want to see. Learn all you can about a destination before you get there. Your interest will be stimulated by knowledge.

Finally, throw away your watch.

■ ■ ■

February 1993

Why a Motorhome?

O ne of the questions most frequently asked of us is, "Why did you choose a motorhome instead of a trailer?" I'm convinced that trying to decide which type of RV to buy is the major question faced by those contemplating the purchase of their first RV. In our case, the decision was made twenty years ago. Now we're on our eleventh motorhome, and we're already planning for the next one.

I don't have any general prejudices against travel trailers or fifth-wheels or, for that matter, truck campers or folding trailers. I like all RVs and believe that there is a place for each type, size, and floorplan. At various stages in our lives, we have owned and used every kind of RV. Each has its special features and fits particular needs, but those needs change during people's lives.

For example, young families with children are usually quite happy with folding trailers, but few full-time retirees opt for that mode. We loved our Apache folding trailer when the kids were small and we actually camped, but, at the present stage in our lives, that type of unit wouldn't serve us well. A motorhome suits us best now.

We drive about 25,000 miles a yearly, usually visiting thirty or more states and spending an average of eight months a year in our rig. That means the largest portion of our lives is spent in our motorhome. Our seminar schedule, which keeps us on the go several months every year, and the people-and-place visits we regularly schedule dictate a great deal of time on the road. That means a lot of stops. Consequently, we are particularly concerned with home comforts, whether in camp or on the road, and with ease of stopping and hooking up. Of the various types of RVs, the motorhome best fills the bill for our requirements.

The fact that you're always inside the RV—whether you are on the road or parked—is a motorhome's first and greatest feature. You (or your passengers) can enjoy its comforts as you travel down the road, including the bathroom, the refrigerator, the sofa, the bed, and other amenities.

I love all the options for motorhomes, many of which can't be installed in trailers. A prime example is leveling jacks. I appreciate pulling into a space, punching one button and, within seconds, becoming perfectly level, with no necessity of carrying a compartment full of wood blocks, no getting my knees dirty while placing the blocks under the wheels, and no aggravation of pulling over the top of those carefully placed blocks. That one option makes hooking up a motorhome so simple and easy.

Another option that I would now have difficulty doing without is a generator. The fact that we can have 115-volt power anytime is a wonderful, practical convenience. It's great to be able to use electrical appliances in air-conditioned comfort, even when parked in the middle of a desert.

Another aspect of motorhoming that I like is that it allows us to use a small car, which we tow everywhere we go. Small cars are less expensive to buy, and they're easy to handle (and park) in city traffic.

Finally, I guess I'm hooked on a feeling described by the late Roger Miller in a song he wrote and recorded many years ago. When I'm tooling down that highway, I feel like I'm "King of the Road."

Yep, motorhoming is partly an emotional choice. But then, isn't most of life, including RVing, based on feelings we derive from the experiences we encounter? And I feel very good just being behind the wheel of a motorhome, wherever that road happens to be taking us.

■ ■ ■

May 1993

Is Now the Time?

A not-infrequent problem among young people is that they act too quickly. On the other hand, older folks sometimes don't act quickly enough. Although there are usually negative consequences in either case, I think the latter can have more significant effects.

This column is addressed particularly to those of you who, like me, are in your senior years. Theoretically, we have reached the stage when we can focus more on activities we freely choose and enjoy, rather than those we must do in order to cope with daily living. But many of us are so conditioned by the many years of struggle to make ends meet that we have difficulty in getting off the dime when we must make major decisions regarding our way of life—or our bank balances! And therein lies the problem. Young folks may have the time to rectify their mistakes, but those of us in our age category may not.

Don't get me wrong. I'm not advocating that conservative retirees suddenly start jumping into all kinds of wild adventures or start buying anything and everything that takes their fancy—regardless of the financial consequences. However, I am suggesting that if we face our limited-time futures realistically, we might be persuaded to take less time to make some of the choices we are faced with. And we might be a little bit more daring in opting for new ways and new things.

My interest in this topic is based primarily on the many conversations I've had with folks who are interested in full-time RVing but can't make up their minds whether or not to tackle it. Some have been considering it for years and are still no closer to a decision than they were at the beginning. I suspect that, in some cases, those folks will still be considering it right up to the end of their time on earth.

There are some things that can't wait. Not that I believe that everyone who thinks about fulltiming should jump into it, disregarding possible consequences. But I do believe that anyone, especially the retiree, who is seriously considering such a change of lifestyle should resolve the question one way or the other relatively quickly.

Another big question that many of us face from time to time is, Should we get a new motorhome? I've talked to people who have been shopping for several years. They usually find models that suit their needs—and pocketbooks— perfectly. The only reason they don't get a new rig is that they can't make that big decision to part with the money.

For those of you who have difficulty in making these decisions, may I recommend a way of looking at things that might help you overcome your indecisiveness? I find it helpful in putting things in a meaningful time framework.

I measure my life every year around birthday time. By that, I mean that I check an insurance company "mortality table," a chart that shows average life expectancy at any given age. In my case, turning sixty-seven last August, I found that I probably have 12.7 years left. If I take a measuring tape and peel it out 67 inches, that is what I have lived. Adding to that the 12.7 that I have left, I peel the tape out to 79.7 inches.

Looking at where I've been and comparing it with where I'm going, the lesson is obvious: At my age, if there are things I want to do or want to get and there are no real reasons for not doing them or getting them, then I'd better get at it.

If you are having difficulty making a major decision, try measuring your life like this. You may decide that now is the time to do whatever it is you've been wanting to do.

■ ■ ■

June 1993

Women's Rights

I n spite of the fact that half of all motorhome users are women, motorhome designers do not give experienced women RVers 50 percent of the influence that goes into motorhome designs. A long-standing problem, it persists even though women have complained about various motorhome design features since the beginning of highway homes. But, unfortunately for the ladies, motorhomes have traditionally been, and still are, primarily the creations "of men, by men and for men."

I draw this conclusion from letters I have received and conversations that I've had with women RVers. Few are totally satisfied with all of the features they have to live and work with. Most oldtimers will admit, however, that things are getting better (for example, microwaves are generally being placed where it doesn't take a basketball player to look inside them). But women still look and hope for more consideration of their needs.

Since I am frequently the cook and housekeeper in our motorhome, I directly encounter the reasons for women's complaints and I have to say, "Ladies, I'm with you." I agree that most of your complaints are not only valid, but in many cases can be reasonably, easily, and inexpensively remedied. Perhaps if all male motorhomers and particularly motorhome designers had to experience some of those inadequacies and inconveniences, they would focus more on livability factors.

Since women usually prepare the food, they are particularly concerned with kitchens and dining areas. A reality for RVing women (especially fulltimers) is that their role in the cooking department changes little from what it was when they had well-equipped kitchens in houses, yet they are expected to make do with less-functional facilities and equipment in motorhomes.

Motorhome kitchens usually don't incorporate all the ease-of-operation features that are possible, particularly when it comes to storage. For example, the large space under the sink is seldom designed for maximum utilization. In most motorhomes, it is either one large space with storage on the bottom, or it contains a shelf midway to create two storage areas. The problem is that both areas are difficult to access easily and effectively. Items stored to the rear—especially on the bottom shelf—are almost impossible to get to without getting down on your hands and knees and removing a number of things.

Another common complaint is that cabinets are too high. Women are generally shorter than men, so cabinets that are easily accessible to men are too high for many women. Although window placement poses a challenge to lowering cabinets because of the necessary concern for light, ventilation, and appearance, I'm sure that many women would cheerfully agree to smaller windows if it meant lower cabinets.

Some miscellaneous complaints that I hear include clothes closets that don't accommodate women's belongings; no laundry hamper; inadequate bathroom drawers for women's things; lack of special places for items such as pictures, books, magazines, knickknacks, etc.; and no provisions for the storage and use of maps, directories, and other materials that copilots pile in front of them as they travel.

I believe that women don't have enough say in how motorhomes are designed. It would be interesting to know how many RV manufacturer have veteran female RVers as designers on their staffs. Until women provide 50 percent of the input at that point, I'd have to say they aren't getting a fair shake.

■ ■ ■

July 1993

Freebie Stops

How often we hear motorhomers say, "I never pay camp-ground fees. When we stop for the night, we just pull into a vacant space: rest stops, shopping center parking lots, wide spots along the road, church parking lots, or wherever we happen to be. We save a lot of money that way."

Yep, it's a good way to save money, but, it's also a way to become a crime statistic. The reality is that the RV lifestyle is relatively crime-free. The RVer who pulls through the gates of a public or private facility can get a good night's rest without fear of becoming a victim. On the other hand, those who use freebie stops where they are accessible to the criminal go to bed with a greater possibility of becoming a crime statistic before morning.

My alarmist feelings are based on the fact that in nearly every case involving crime against RVers, the act occurred at an isolated place. Generally, that place is a rest stop. It may be a fact that criminals aren't in campgrounds, but it's equally factual that many criminals are on the highways and in the cities. Thus, RVers who turn in for the night at rest stops and shopping center parking lots are on the bad guys' turf. Several robbery/murders occurred at rest stops in recent years, yet I know of no serious crimes in campgrounds or RV parks.

Other than the danger involved there's another reason for not camp-ing at some of the popular freebie stops: It may be illegal. An RVer may find himself awakened in the middle of the night to sign a ticket. Many parking lots have signs posted stating that overnight parking violates city ordinances. Again, there is the chance of a rude awakening in the middle of the night and a citation.

My point is, it may be dangerous or illegal to use some of the commonly used freebie stopping places. However, that does not mean there aren't places where one can park a motorhome overnight that are both legal and safe, and just as available.

Truck stops! Thousands of them dot our highways, and they are becoming havens for the RVer who just wants to pull off the road without the time and trouble of checking in at a campground or RV park.

All industries constantly seek new sources of revenue, and the truck-stop industry apparently is beginning to target RVers. In recent months on our annual tour of some two dozen states, we've seen several indications of that interest in the RVer. In South Carolina, a truckstop's billboard offered: FREE PARKING FOR TRUCKS AND RVs. Our own *Trucker's Friend* listing of truck stops and their services includes a category of "RV Services." Some have a special parking area for RVs so truck noise may be reduced considerably. Of course, there is some truck noise all night long, but the tired traveler will snooze right through it. On the plus side, what better place to stop for fuel than at the big stalls most truck stops have Most of the newer, modern truck stops offer a multitude of services that RVers can choose from: minimarts, phones, restaurants, gifts, etc. In short, some of those truck stops fill a variety of RVers' needs all in one place.

However, lest anyone interpret from my remarks that I've become an advocate of truck-stop camping, let me assure you that I haven't. I would prefer to be inside a park with hookups, away from highway noise. I sleep better that way.

But on those occasional times when I have to drive long and late to be at a certain place at a certain time, I'll continue to do my freebie camping where I feel safe and welcome—at truck stops.

■ ■ ■

August 1993

Books and Places

Visits to the wonderful places available to motorhomers provide us with grand experiences. Supplementing what we see with good reading about those locations enhances the total experience.

In my case, perhaps a background as a history student and a teacher makes me more avid about visiting historical places than other people. However, I notice that I always have plenty of company at most of them, and I'm sure those folks weren't all history teachers. Quite simply, places that portray or reveal our past are of interest to most Americans.

When planning a trip I always study the route we will be traveling, looking for special places to visit; sometimes we select places first, then plan the route. In either case, before we take off, we bone up on those special places. That way we always have a background on what we see.

I've been hooked on the West for most of my adult life and never miss opportunities to learn more. I'm particularly fond of southwestern history, especially if it concerns famous outlaws and lawmen. But it's difficult to separate fact from fiction if one merely reads the scanty information that is given on signs, plaques, or brochures at most historical places. That's where I find it useful to do my homework before I visit those sites.

An example of one of the most interesting and satisfactory trips we've ever taken was a visit to the Tularosa Valley in New Mexico. A dozen or more years ago, I read a fascinating book about the trials and tribulations of the early settlers of that area. Last fall, when we were planning a trip to the East, I decided to route us through that valley in order to actually see the town of Tularosa and learn more about some of the people and events I had read about. Just before we left, I reread the book to better fix some of the characters and places in my mind.

To our good fortune, not only did we encounter fabulous weather and scenery in the Tularosa Valley, but we found the owner/manager of the KOA where we stayed, Ken Bonnell, was born and reared in Tularosa. An enthusiastic amateur historian, he loves to show off his hometown. A walking tour with running commentary on people and events of his childhood kept us enthralled. (Many of these stories are recounted in an unpublished manuscript available in his campground store.) I was particularly excited to hear that one of the young cowboys who was accused of murder and chased by the famous sheriff and killer of Billy the Kid, Pat Garrett, was "Uncle Jim" to my guide!

The point is that my book knowledge of the area enabled me to enjoy the region much more than I would have, had I not had that knowledge.

Another way to mix books and places is to visit the latter first. The seeing can be the stimulus that leads to a desire to know the story more fully. Frequently, I read biographies of people who figured in events that occurred at the places we visit. In the case of many historical places, excellent books are sold in gift shops. Also, I find that tourist bureaus and chambers of commerce usually have brochures and booklets that provide good information. Of course, a frustrating aspect of seeing first and reading later is that a book will frequently provide information that would have been useful if you had it when you were visiting the place.

But regardless of what order you prefer, I urge all readers to do both. The joy of visiting one of the special places for the first time is a great experience. Getting more detailed information about it can make that experience even more satisfying.

Books and places go together.

■ ■ ■

September 1993

Lessons from the Heart

O n Good Friday, at the Wild West Samboree at Sacramento, California, I had the pleasure of presenting my full-timing seminar to a wonderfully receptive crowd. As is my custom, I ended the session with a gimmick intended to get folks to think seriously about their priorities for the immediate future—especially lifestyle plans such as fulltiming.

As I explained once before in an earlier column, I measure my life in inches by slowly peeling out a rolled-up tape measure. At age sixty-seven, it takes a lot of tape to show the years I've lived. According to insurance statistics, I have only twelve years left—a short piece of tape compared with the sixty-seven that represent years past. Thus my purpose is illustrated: Time is running out, so give special thought as to how to spend those remaining years.

It's a performance—or was, until that fateful Good Friday a few weeks ago when two hours after the seminar, I found myself riding in an ambulance to Mercy Hospital. Prompt examination showed that I had blocked arteries, 90 percent on the major one. In short, I could be dead at any moment.

I won't dwell on the grim particulars, except to say that a five-bypass procedure was performed and that I am well on the way to recovery. In fact, the doctors say that I will be better than new in three months. But the old ball game is mine again to play in whatever way I choose. I've already made some important decisions on some new rules.

Don't ignore warning signs. I did and I regret it. For six months, after exertion, I felt a heaviness in my chest that I ascribed to being out of shape and, very simply, getting old. I considered checking with a doctor, but being on the road, that meant picking one at random some where. I just kept putting it off until I could see our family doctor.

Listen to your spouse. Margie is a registered nurse, so I don't usually complain to her unless I really hurt. However, I did tell her several times about my exhaustion, and she urged me to check into an emergency room at several places. But I refused to go, still blaming the problem on my lack of exercise, on the promise to see our family doctor immediately upon arrival at home.

Don't pile on extra weight. I gained about fifteen extra pounds this past winter. Unfortunately, the opportunities to dine out had been numerous in recent months, and I stuffed myself with all kinds of things that I shouldn't have: lots of fried foods; racks of barbecued ribs; gobs of butter on hot rolls; potatoes loaded with sour cream; and oodles of pies, cakes, and other delicacies, including daily candy and cashew snacks.

Exercise regularly. I found every excuse in the world not to exercise daily. For years, Margie and I have had a morning regimen that included a brisk two-mile walk, or we used our cross-country skier. For some unexplainable reason, last winter we found more excuses not to exercise than we found in the previous five years.

In short, all the lessons were there and all were obvious. I was headed for a heart attack and was too dumb to accept the realities. I know many people who ignore the warnings. They jokingly exempt themselves from the statistics, the realities, and believe it's only something that happens to someone else.

Take it from someone who has been there: There's no greater enjoyment than life. Stare the alternative in the eyeballs for a few minutes and you'll understand what I mean.

And, like some of you, I believe there are "exemptions." But is it worth the risk to believe that you are one of them?

■ ■ ■

November 1993

If We Had Known Then . . .

How many things most of us would have done differently if we had only known then what we know now! I've lived my life generally the way I wanted to, but there are times when I've wished for another shot at something I've done. And I have plenty of company with my wishing.

How often I've heard enthusiastic fulltimers say that they wished they had started sooner. Unfortunately, some of them have waited so long to hit the road that their time is now limited by health problems and advancing age. I can recall times, when I was an RV dealer, that customers who were well into their sixties or early seventies would tell me about their dreams of fulltiming—but they still couldn't make up their minds on whether or not to try it! It made me want to scream at them, "For heaven's sake, go now before it's too late!" I'm sure many of them were later to voice those rueful words, "If we had only known then . . ."

I'd like to have a dollar for every time I've heard motorhome owners lament the fact that they were too conservative, too frugal when they selected the rig they now have. "If we had known then how important an extra three feet would be—or a separate bedroom, or leveling jacks, or a bigger engine, or a second air conditioner—we would have gotten it to begin with."

Often the reason motorhomers buy a second rig is to get the features they rejected the first time in order to save money. Most motorhome buyers could have done a better job of buying if they had put more investigation and common sense into their buying preparations. A choice that was intended to save money actually ends up at times costing much more and includes the sorrowful feeling that goes with the comment, "If we had only known then . . . "

A not-uncommon regret of older folks who have been conservative and timid in their approach to motorhoming is that they didn't act more daring in their travels, didn't follow more blue lines on their maps, didn't try more side roads. Too late they realize that by being sensible and practical, they missed some great experiences. "Ah, if they had only known then . . . "

I look back on over three decades of RVing and have some regrets that we didn't arrange to take our grandkids and our parents with us on more trips. Margie's dad particularly liked to travel. We took him (and Grandma) with us on Good Sam's first tour of Baja. Looking back, it is obvious that the adventure was special to them—and us. One of our most memorable trips included two granddaughters when they were eleven and thirteen. We had six wonderful weeks with them. I wish we had taken them more—before they discovered boys! "If we had known then what we know now . . . "

The fact is we'll all give up RVing some day: some will voluntarily and others will be forced to. Among the latter are undoubtedly those who haven't tried some variations of motorhoming that they've thought about now and then, but for various reasons never got around to, like boondocking, for example. Many RVers do it, but many just talk about it and never seem to quite put it together. Or spending a winter in Mexico. Or taking some of the exciting escorted tours like the piggyback train through Copper Canyon. Or barging down the Mississippi. Many of us intend to do all these things someday. But I wonder which of us will never get around to it and end up regretfully saying, "If I had only known then . . . "

Perhaps all of us should work a little harder on happy foresight so we won't have to spend so much time on rueful hindsight.

■ ■ ■

December 1993

Meeting Life Halfway

The ideal view of motorhoming is one of exciting places, scenic wonders, and congenial companions. The reality is there are days when the weather is gloomy, the terrain tedious, and the motorhoming couple have only each other (one of whom may be grumpy) for company.

At times like the latter, we are put to the test of making do in circumstances that are less than ideal. Anyone who has experienced three consecutive days of torrential downpours, in the midst of a lake-like third-rate campground with no cable television and no shopping malls within fifty miles, knows what I mean. The term *compatibility* has real significance for the motorhome's occupants at those times.

Recently, I visited friends at their motorhome during a rain that had been going on for several days. When they opened their door for me, I noticed both had books in their hands. As avid readers with a plentiful supply of reading material, they simply used the time to pursue one of their favorite pastimes. I can relate to their enjoyment of those times, since both Margie and I always have books under way and no day passes without some reading. Consequently, we are never bored when outside conditions are bad and attractions are few. In fact, we even look forward to afternoons with our books, when we can just sit under our awning reading while the sun beams brightly.

For those who aren't into reading, there are dozens of spare-time activities compatible with motorhoming. The point is this: All motorhomers who spend a lot of time in their rigs should have something that makes cooped-up time interesting. It doesn't make a great deal of difference what that activity is as long as all occupants of the motorhome either enjoy it or are satisfied with the other person(s) doing it.

Exercise buffs who regularly take long walks, run, or ride bicycles, and those who must always be on the go find motorhoming difficult at times. One of my special friends is an avid sportsman—golf and tennis—and he's one of those hypergoers who has to be involved in something very active or exciting at all times. He isn't a reader or a TV watcher, nor does he have an activity that can be pursued in his motorhome. Inclement weather makes life difficult for him. He just can't stand inactivity and lack of excitement. Consequently, he goes bonkers whenever he's cooped up.

Another low-key activity that is pursued by many motorhomers in foul weather (or fair) is the art of conversation. Most motorhomers have a more than ample supply of gregariousness genes and enjoy visiting with their neighbors. With the infinite variety of people who motorhome, what a wonderful opportunity the lifestyle offers the people-curious person. As one of that type, I relish meeting people all over the United States and hearing their stories.

Motorhomers who travel a lot usually try to follow scenic roads. Fortunately, most maps designate scenic highways so it's quite easy to plot a course that takes you through special countrysides. However, the reality is that many roads can be quite devoid of beautiful nature. It is in those instances that those who are curious enough to look for and see something interesting where most folks don't are indeed fortunate. If you look carefully, there's always something worth noticing, a bird, a windmill, a faraway ranch, or just a winding dirt road.

Life isn't always a bundle of excitement. Motorhoming is no exception. But it can always be interesting. You've just got to meet real life halfway.

■ ■ ■

January 1994

What Options?

A buyer of a new motorhome is faced with an intimidating number of choices in selecting a make, model, and size. But even after that difficult selection has been made, he is faced with an almost-equal task in choosing the options.

Options can constitute a significant portion of the total cost of a new motorhome. The smart buyer will peruse the list of "goodies" carefully and give a lot of thought about what to include and what to leave off. Some buyers make the mistake of not getting everything they really need to make their dreams come true, while others waste money by taking expensive options they never use. Either way, the mistake can be avoided if proper consideration is given before the purchase order is signed. Obviously, the solution to both problems is to make the right decision at the right time. And therein lies the dilemma.

What options do I really need? In my seminar on "Choosing the Right RV," I deal with that frequently asked question. Although I can't actually tell people what they specifically need, I do strongly advise them to understand the need to make their choices before they finalize their motorhome purchase. I offer two reasons for that: (1) options can usually be installed better during the manufacturing process (e.g., leveling jacks are easy to install on the bare rails of a chassis, but difficult on a completed motorhome); and (2) the job can be done less expensively because of cheaper labor costs at that time.

My advice to buyers is this: Buy every option you like at the time you buy the motorhome unless there is a reason not to. Please note that I did not say buy everything; I said that you should buy everything you like—unless there is a reason not to. Review the option list carefully and ask yourselves about each item:

"Do I want this?" If the answer is yes, and there is no reason not to get it, then certainly that is the time to include that item in your order. Try to avoid spoiling your trips by always wishing for options you don't have and end up paying a lot more for when you do get them.

Personally, we like about every option that manufacturers offer. When I am asked what I consider the most important, I have to answer that it depends on the individual. For example, we like and frequently use our combination washer/dryer; however, I know that many RVers would not. To us, it is such a convenience to keep caught up on the laundry by doing small loads every two or three days rather than saving up a couple of machine loads and doing them at a campground laundry. Because it fits our particular way of living in a motorhome, we would definitely list this option among our top choices.

Basic options that we would never want to be without are air conditioners (both front and rear), a generator, an awning (plus window awnings), two televisions (we are bedtime TV watchers), a microwave oven (Margie loves her new convection/microwave combo), the largest refrigerator available, leveling jacks (never, never again do I want to go through stair-step building with wooden blocks), and, with a diesel engine, an exhaust brake.

We use all of the above-listed options on a regular basis. They make our motorhoming comfortable. To us, they have become necessities and, fortunately, we can scrape up the cash to have them. However, we can clearly remember the old days when we could not afford such luxuries. But we still had a great time regardless of what we had. After all, it's the motorhoming experiences that count most, not the motorhome.

■ ■ ■

February 1994
Getting Fixed

I'm sure that, like me, most oldtime motorhomers have the cockles of their hearts warmed each year when they see the fabulous new models with their marvelous features. I'm equally certain that, like me, most of those oldtimers who become owners of new rigs soon discover that these wonderful new machines aren't perfect and may still have to be fixed—sometimes more frequently than their less-sophisticated predecessors. And that fact leads to feelings that range all the way from aggravating for the good mechanic, to disturbing and terrifying for those of us who can barely differentiate between a monkey and the wrench with the same name.

I have noted over the years that many motorhomers love to work on their machines. They frequently work on them simply because they are skilled craftsmen who enjoy fixing things—even things that may not be broken! These motorhomers usually have picture-perfect rigs, and they take pleasure in showing their handiwork to those of us who are less skilled.

The fellow who is a skilled mechanic, metalworker, plumber, carpenter, electrician, and general all-around craftsman usually carries a great toolbox with him in his motorhome. When something needs fixing, he simply takes out the appropriate tool and solves the problem. For those of us who aren't skilled in all of the trades, we have to approach our dilemmas differently. I'll share with you my special way of solving breakdown problems as I travel.

Like the expert craftsman, I carry a well-stocked toolbox. But from there on, I use my head instead of my hands to get things fixed. I call my approach the "Maxwell Head-Scratch Method." Here's how it works.

Scenario: You're in a campground or RV park or somewhere with other RVers. Something has broken on your rig. Stand in front of the broken part, stare at it with a puzzled look on your face and scratch your head. Pretty soon one of those real competent, mechanically minded fellows will come along. Nine times out of ten, he can't resist asking a puzzled-looking guy who's scratching his head, "What's the matter?" With total bewilderment in your voice, you answer, "Something is broken. I don't know how to fix it."

Now, none of these Mr. Fix-it guys can resist that kind of challenge. As surely as rain is wet, he'll ask, "Mind if I take a look at it?" and start crawling underneath your rig or doing whatever is required to get to the problem.

Now here's where you and your toolbox come into the picture. Shortly, from under the rig, you'll hear something like, "Do you have a ⁹⁄₁₆ box-end wrench?"

At that instant, it is important for you to answer with a very positive response. "I sure do. Right here." And you grab that wrench fast and hand it to him before he gets a chance to come out to go to his toolbox, and in the process realize what he's doing and change his mind about helping you! By all means, keep him under there until he finishes the job. Then when he comes out smiling—that see-how-smart-I-am smile—have a clean rag for him to wipe his hands on and offer him a cold beer. Be sure to tell him how much you appreciate and admire his wonderful skill and willingness to assist a dummy like you.

The point is that a lot of motorhomers are very competent with tools. Many are the neighborly type who don't mind giving a helping hand to those who don't have their talents. All you need to do is get their attention with a magic gesture that invites them to show their stuff—and then scratch! Scratch!

■ ■ ■

Having Your Cake ...

A piece of tongue-in-cheek advice that I give prospective full-timers in my seminars is this: "The first thing you do to prepare for fulltiming is to create 365 friends well scattered throughout the United States." Audiences catch on quickly that I am facetiously suggesting a very inexpensive (cheap?) way to RV around the country. (Think about it, though—one night a year with each friend, free space, no doubt an excellent dinner, probably breakfast. The plan has great possibilities!)

We find that visiting relatives and friends from the comfort of our own home adds to the enjoyment of those get-togethers. Much of the work and disruption for those having company, and for those being guests, is lessened. When we tell friends and relatives we're going to visit them, they know they don't have to start rearranging their houses and lives to accommodate us.

On our pre-RV days, overnight visits meant dragging our stuff into someone's house where there never seemed to be quite enough room for everything. And it meant sleeping in a strange bed, one with pillows that didn't feel like mine. Usually it meant sharing a bathroom, a situation that really bugs me.

No matter how considerate your hosts may be, they generally do things their way, and you are more or less compelled to follow suit. You get up when they do; you eat when they serve meals; you eat what they serve (prepared their way, of course); you follow their lead in how you spend your time; and, the most distressing situation of all, you must defer to the hosts in their domination of the TV remote control! If they want to watch *Roseanne* when your preference would be a ball game, guess what? You must graciously watch what your hosts prefer while your favorite team goes on to victory or defeat without your viewing support.

On the other hand, when parked in your hosts' driveway, you can enjoy your visiting pretty much on your own terms. You sleep in your own bed with your own pillow, find your toothbrush in its accustomed place, and enjoy your own special TV programs. Your clothes and other things are where you generally keep them. In short, although you are visiting, you still remain essentially in your own bailiwick. It's really having your cake and eating it too.

While visiting friends as you travel via motorhome has some pluses, there are some minuses. For example, lacking good advance information about your hosts' location and parking facilities can lead you to winding uphill on narrow streets, only to discover that your intended parking space is several feet shorter than your rig. I made this mistake and ended up backtracking several miles to an RV park. Henceforth, before I venture into a strange area to visit folks, especially those who live in hilly cities, I will make a trial run in my car. It may be a bit of trouble, but not nearly as much as the predicament in which I recently found myself.

Another "minus" situation that you sometimes encounter is that your visit reaches a stage where you would like to retreat to your motorhome, but can't figure out how to make an exit without offending your hosts. A surefire excuse that can't possibly meet with objection is this: You look at your watch and exclaim, "Oh, it's time for my pill. And since it's getting late and we're tired, and I know you folks must be exhausted from entertaining us so wonderfully, we'll just turn in early." Who can tell you that you don't need your pill?

Incidentally, tonight as I write this, we're staying in an RV park for the first time in several days. No friends or relatives in Lordsburg, New Mexico—darn it!

■ ■ ■

April 1994

Motorhome Manners

As far as I know, Emily Post didn't write a chapter for motor-homing. However, that doesn't mean there aren't some rules of etiquette that we should follow as we tool our leviathans around the highways and byways.

The fact is, because of our mode of living/transportation, we are very conspicuous. It follows that we are criticized more frequently than folks in normal-sized vehicles. Since it is definitely better that we, as a group, portray a positive image of our lifestyle, it behooves us to always be on our best behavior when we're on the road. Like it or not, we are very much on display.

A perfect example of what I am saying is the much-publicized episode of the motorhomer whose burning tire started forest fires in Idaho. Whether or not the motorhomer was at fault is beside the point; the reality is that a lot of publicity about motorhomers was generated, and some of it portrays us as a group of stubborn old fools. Had the vehicle involved been only an automobile would there have been the national publicity that ensued? Of course not. But the fact that it was a big motorhome chugging its way up a mountain road conjures up memories in the minds of many car drivers of similar situations when they were held back by slow-moving RVs. Unfortunately, it's an image that an awful lot of people can relate to.

Important though our image may be, there's even a better reason for motorhomers to adhere to a set of good manners on the highway: safety. The former leads directly to the latter. I'd like to review some of the common road courtesies that I all too frequently see motor-homers fail to extend—practices that are also dangerous.

Tailgating. It's surprising how often I see a motorhome driver hanging right on to the bumper of another vehicle. Not only does it upset the occupants of the car in front to se the monster at their heels, but it creates a real danger for everyone. Every motorhome driver should know how difficult it is to stop his rig and leave plenty of stopping room between himself and the car in front of him.

Failing to yield a lane. Even the most even-tempered auto driver becomes a bit upset when he is unable to pass a slower-moving car because a motorhome is blocking the faster lane. Hogging the faster lanes when the right lane is open is a clear violation of highway etiquette and, in most cases, the law.

Cutting in too quickly. A motorhome towing a car needs a lot of road to clear a vehicle it is passing.

Not giving a courtesy blink to an overtaking vehicle. In spite of the controversy about truck drivers, I find that the majority of them are both courteous and safety-conscious with motorhomers. Almost invariably they will give you a courtesy blink when you are safely clear after overtaking one.

Not pulling over for faster vehicles on hills. This is one of the worst-case scenarios involving RVs. It's just a fact that our rigs don't go uphill as fast as cars do. We all find ourselves at times on mountain roads with cars behind us wanting to get around. The stubborn motorhome driver who loves to pile them up behind and then give the bird to those who shout at him when they finally get around is a discredit to all of us. Though it may be inconvenient to pull over, we should do so as soon as possible, even if it means coming to a complete stop.

Since these points of etiquette are quite elementary, readers might wonder why I rehash them. The answer is simple. I drove 472 miles on Interstate 75 today. I saw each and every one of those rules violated.

Need I say more?

■ ■ ■

May 1994

The Melting Pot

America has long been described as a melting pot for people who come here from scores of countries around the world. They arrive as Germans, Frenchmen, Hungarians, Italians, or whatever, but in the process of living here they become Americans.

And so it is with motorhomers. We enter the lifestyle as doctors, lawyers, plumbers, carpenters, preachers, teachers, laborers, farmers, (even writers), but basically what we were is unimportant in our new and very unique social setting. Now we are identified simply as motorhomers.

A wonderful aspect of RVing is that the lifestyle discourages social classification. Some adherents may be wealthy and were higher-ups in the business world. Some may have rigs that cost a lot of money. Some may have Ph.D.s. But none of those factors necessarily enables these folks to savor more thoroughly the delights and benefits of RVing than the common man who has an inexpensive rig and a modest bank account. The sun beams just as warmly, the birds sing just as cheerfully, the mountains appear just as magnificent, and the neighbors are just as friendly to people of modest means, education, and social position. In short, all motorhomers are melted down into a very special group dedicated to enjoying the many special attractions of this land and the people in it.

For example, I'm writing this from one of our favorite winter haunts (River Ranch, Florida, on December 31), and Margie and I have just returned from our daily two-mile walk. During that walk, we met dozens of people, some of whom we have become acquainted with during our stay here or in previous visits, but most of whom were total strangers. Yet we all greeted each other cheerfully as if we were friends.

I'm sure that if we had the opportunity to meet for longer periods of time some of them would become friends. It's just a matter of communication, and people who communicate usually get along.

Motorhomers are generally good communicators. The lifestyle encourages interaction—quick interaction. The fact that we can be here today and gone tomorrow encourages us to get to know our neighbors quickly.

Of course what we did, where we lived, what we have and what we know are not as obvious in an RV park or campground as in "normal life." Out of our regular lifestyle there are fewer social marking to create social classes. So we all get lumped together and melted down into a common group.

Yes, there are differences among us. But other than our rigs, there are few of them that categorize RVers socially. Even the rig factor is relatively slight. Common interests, experiences, and problems make us alike more than the differences in our vehicles differentiate us.

It's New Year's Eve tonight and we're going to a party. We know many of the folks who will be there. We don't know what all of them did for a living, how long they went to school, how much money they have in the bank, or how big their houses are or were. But we do know that we all will be dressed about the same (casual); our taste buds will run about the same (unfortunately unstated, due to no-fat, no-cholesterol, no-sodium diets), our conversation will be on subjects of mutual interest (kids, grandkids and RVs) and we'll reminisce, share stories, and laugh as we sit around the fire.

So although our backgrounds might be diverse, and at one time we may have been in a variety of social classes, now, as motorhomers, we are pretty much alike. We've been melted down.

June 1994

Good Eating Tips

Readers may recall that several months ago I had my old ticker overhauled (five bypasses). Until I became a heart-surgery victim, I was unaware of the "zipper club," which I discovered to have hundreds of thousands of members. Not only do we all have in common the fact that we have endured radical surgery, but we share a cheerless future at the dining table. In short, we diet or we die.

As a product of the Midwest during the Depression years, I grew up on a diet of what are now considered the wrong things. Much of what we ate was laced with fat (fried) or laden with sugar (as in pies and cakes) or loaded with cholesterol (I never heard that dirty word until I was middle-aged).

But after over sixty years of generally pleasurable eating, it all came to a skidding halt. Like all my fellow zipper-club members, I have been warned to change my way of eating or be prepared to suffer the knife and saw again in the near future.

While receiving checkout instructions from my doctor, I made the observation and inquiry: "It took me sixty-seven years to stop up. Does that mean that if I return to my old way of eating that I have another sixty-seven to go before it happens again?"

My doctor's very emphatic response was, "No, that's not the way it works." He then introduced me to a book called *The New American Diet*. Life at mealtimes hasn't been the same since.

The good news is: I feel great—lots of energy, good blood pressure, and no bellyaches. I'm toting fifteen fewer pounds than before the surgery (back into some of those size 36 pants that I've been saving), I enjoy my walks, and the Tagamet bottle hasn't been emptied in a long time.

But there's bad news, too. Mealtimes are frequently bad times. The "what's-good-for-me" book (and Margie) tell me what's good for me, but my taste buds disagree about what is good. The aroma of bacon or sausage that floats through the morning air in campgrounds as I march through my two-mile daily health-walk sets the old blood-pump to percolating, but it also excites my salivary glands unmercifully, especially since I can only look forward to breakfast fare consisting of cornflakes with skim milk.

Meals at home aren't too bad. Margie gets aggravated at my failure to become ecstatic about broccoli, carrots, and cauliflower. But her imagination has no bounds when it comes to preparing chicken.

Some of my RV buddies have learned ways to cancel the negative aspects of some of the foods that are bad for you:

- Broken cookies don't have nearly the calories of whole cookies.
- Waffles that float in syrup may obviously be called "lite."
- A raw parsnip (a turnip may be substituted) eaten after a bowl of ice cream kills the fat.
- Turning a steak often (a minimum of six times) while it is on the grill shakes the fat out.
- Microwaving pie for 10 to 15 seconds radiates out calories and other harmful substances.
- The calories in alcoholic beverages are reduced by half if you sip your drink slowly (one teaspoonful at a sip taken at one-minute intervals).
- Brown eggs fried in an iron skillet have reduced cholesterol.
- A dinner of fried chicken, gravy, and mashed potatoes is okay if you also eat at least four green vegetables.

I'm sure there are other diet secrets that I haven't heard about, but I keep my ears open. After all, where my health is concerned, I want the best advice I can get.

■ ■ ■

July 1994
Warts and All

I
n my writings and seminars, I almost invariably paint a good picture of the motorhoming lifestyle. In that picture the participants are enjoying beautiful America, fascinating places, exciting events, wonderful gourmet foods, and perfectly delightful fellow travelers. In short, all is hearts, flowers, and tiddlywinks.

But is that a true picture? Unfortunately, I must admit that it sometimes isn't. The reality is that we have those times when everything seems to go wrong, such as when the motorhome breaks down on a yucky day in a yucky place. Times when even the most mild-tempered of us (Margie probably disagrees with the inclusion of myself in that category) is inclined to be a bit crabby.

We are on the road eight months a year and average about 25,000 miles during that time. As might be expected, we encounter all kinds of societal and natural situations and conditions. Consequently, we experience our share of problems.

Because of my practice of getting a new motorhome every other year, we have the additional aggravation of the debugging process that is almost guaranteed with all new rigs. And that means frequent visits to RV repair shops. In fact, we've spent so much time in them that I'm considering writing a book titled *Life in RV Repair Shops*. (It'll be a thick book!) I'd hate to count the nights we've "camped" beside repair facilities—sometimes inside. Those nights give you lots of time to wonder why is it that your rig is never done when promised? Or, worse yet, why is it that you all too often have to go back because a job wasn't done right the first time?

And then there's bad weather that hits all of us at times. Even the most avid sun-chasers have to take their share of lumps from Old Man Weather. We get more than our share, that's our fault. Due to our seminar schedule that can sometimes have us where we shouldn't be from a weather standpoint, we occasionally find ourselves in a fix. For example, we recently had to drive through Kentucky in a snow and sleet storm. And just last week we drove through central Louisiana in rain so heavy the windshield wipers couldn't keep up. I can still almost feel the shivers and jerks of the motorhome as violent gusts pounded its side all through New Mexico last spring. And a couple of years ago we awakened at the Timonium, Maryland, show with a 5-inch-deep white coating on our rig. I can honestly say that motorhoming under these conditions is not exactly a joyous experience.

But in spite of the aggravations that result from mechanical problems, the sometimes-trying effect of getting things fixed, and the disagreeable weather, we haven't given up our lifestyle. We've learned to take the bad with the good, and there's a heck of a lot more of the latter. For every day we've spent in repair shops, there have been months when we've been trouble-free. For every hour of perverse nature we've suffered through, we've enjoyed weeks of glorious sunshine and balmy breezes. You have to look at the big picture and focus on all good things rather than the bad.

On the practical side, take good care of your rig; it pays off. Proper maintenance and careful treatment go a long way toward keeping breakdowns to a minimum. As far as adverse weather is concerned, Horace Greeley once said, "Go south, man, and stay there all winter," or something like that.

Motorhoming may not be the perfect way to enjoy life in the United States, but it's the best I know— warts and all!

■ ■ ■

August 1994

Getting and Giving

It is my custom to personally and promptly answer all letters addressed to me. I always enjoy hearing from readers, especially those who agree with and are complimentary about the things I've written.

However, I pay particular attention to negative criticism because I try above all to deal with the diverse aspects of the RV lifestyle as accurately and meaningfully as possible. When someone writes to point out that I have made what they consider incorrect observations, I try to look at all sides. Sometimes I even change my mind. But usually those criticisms indicate only that there are many and varied views about RVing and all are correct or incorrect according to the viewer.

In either case, I appreciate the time and effort readers take to express their opinions. That's why I always answer mail.

However, I received a letter recently that frustrates me because I can't answer it directly. The writer, a lady in Lakeland, Florida, didn't give her name or address. Since the criticism she makes of my recent column "Getting Fixed" accuses me of advocating freeloading on the talents and generosity of fellow RVers, I want to set the record straight.

In her letter, Mrs. No Name "sees red" because "some of the guys in this RV park are just like you. They stand outside scratching their heads until my husband, Mr. Fix-it, does their work for them."

About one of their neighbors she says, "He goes to Camping World weekly, brings all kinds of things home, then stands and scratches his head until my husband installs things for him. My husband calls that guy dumb, but he isn't dumb; he's smart. He gets his work done free."

But what she objects to most is that the people her husband helps never respond by "bringing a pizza over some evening or offering to buy a hamburger sometime to repay for all the work."

Well, Mrs. No Name, the reality is that I am very much an anti-free-loader. However, I am a staunch advocate of giving kind-hearted, help-thy-neighbor types ample opportunity to satisfy their penchant for doing good deeds. That means of course, that when I'm baffled about a broken or malfunctioning part on my motorhome and show it by scratching my head, and do-gooders volunteer to fix things, I feel that I have done them a favor by stepping aside and letting them show me their talents. How else will they get to express their generous natures and show their wonderful skills unless we "dummies" give them opportunities?

But I do agree strongly with you, Mrs. No Name, that I should also demonstrate my generous nature and show my appreciation for good deeds by offering tangible tokens, for example, pizzas, hamburgers, or suitable liquids.

Freeloaders who take advantage of generous folks are near the top of my unfavorite people. Whether it be freeloaders of other people's time and talents or the cheapskates who come to potlucks with stale vanilla wafers, it's all the same. Fortunately, RVers in that category are the minority and are soon discovered.

On the other hand, if you or your husband expect payment for volunteer work, then those expectations should be made clear in the beginning. In short, offer professional services, not good neighborliness.

One of the marvelous features of the RV lifestyle is that most of us give and take freely. We help when we can; we accept help when we need to. In either case, it should be done in a friendly, neighborly spirit.

What goes around should come around.

■ ■ ■

November 1994

The Travel Bug

Like the early bird seeking a worm, avid RVers are always on the lookout for new places to go. Some of the ideas come at the darnedest times and from the most unexpected sources—like recently, when I was watching the morning news and a government official who was a public beach expert was being interviewed.

From that program, I learned that there are 650 public beaches on the U.S. coastline and that three of the top five (in his judgment) were on the Gulf Coast of Florida. Two of those five, Grayton and St. Andrews, are state parks on the coast of the Panhandle. Grabbing one of my ever-present atlases, I quickly pinpointed both places. And almost at that instant, I set one of our goals for this winter's ramblings.

Florida has been a destination for us for the past half-dozen or so winters. One of our reasons for going there is that we enjoy the usually great weather. Another is that we do our seminar program at the Tampa RV Show in January.

We have been through the Panhandle many times, but I can recall stopping overnight on the coast only once. Usually we're on our way to some place out west, and we're barreling down Interstate 10 toward Texas or Arizona or California. But this year will be different.

As I pored over my maps, I planned a trip that will actually start at Mobile, Alabama, and follow Route 98 to where it curves to the south. Included in the route are both Grayton and St. Andrews Beach state parks. And I see lots of other interesting-looking places marked on the maps. We'll visit those too, and, no doubt, we'll learn of a lot of other special places during the weeks (or months) that we're there.

I do recall the two nights we spent at a campground at Panacea several years ago. We were parked next to a couple from Illinois who go to that campground every winter. They had been oystering when we arrived and had come in with a huge catch. Like a magnet, those oysters lured us over to their motorhome. Margie, who just loves raw oysters, gorged on the slimy little things, while I chatted with the couple. We had to decline an invitation to cross the road and go shrimping the next day because we needed to move on. Now, I just love shrimp, so I guarantee you that since we won't be in a hurry this winter that I will do a bit of gorging on those tattle bugs.

Fortunately, my interest in history has rubbed off on Margie, and we enjoy visiting historical sites. We have quite a few on our list of must-sees, including Fort Pickens, the Wesley House and Eden State Gardens, St. Mark's Lighthouse, and the town of Apalachicola, to name a few. Road signs will lure us off the main highways time after time.

One would think that after more than three decades of touring the country that our ardor for travel would be somewhat diminished. We've been in all forty-eight contiguous states many times; we've crisscrossed the country more times than I can remember; and we've spent most of our time for the past fifteen years on the road. A pretty close estimate of our road miles would have to be in excess of a half-million.

Logically, we should be tired of travel. But you know what? I think we are just as excited about this Florida coast trip as we were when we planned our first RV trip in 1954. And that's the key to successful motorhoming. If you keep your curiosity level up, your excitement level will follow.

When that travel bug bit us a long time ago, he clamped his jaws real hard. And he's still hangin' on 'cause we're still looking for new places to go.

■ ■ ■

Never Too Old

L ast week I did something I had never done before. To celebrate my sixty-ninth birthday, I went to a horse race. In spite of
the fact that I am a total greenhorn about horse racing, I bet on
every race. And much to my surprise, not only did I have a great time,
but I won a bundle (well not really a big bundle, sort of a little bundle—
$28 to be exact).

The main point, though, is that I tried something new and had a
great time. Undoubtedly much of the fun was due to the fact that I was
with a gang of relatives, and we always have a good time at our reunions.
However, although I'm not much of a gambler, I must confess that
my adrenaline count went off the chart as the nags pounded down
the home stretch—especially when my horse was near the front. Like a
true race nut, I waved my arms and yelled like a banshee.

I don't know why it took me so long to get around to going to a horse
race. I've been asked many times but somehow it just never struck my
fancy. I guess I have the fault that so many folks have too often: passing
up opportunities to enjoy new things simply because we're comfortable
in our ruts. I wonder how often we cheat ourselves out of good times
when we do that.

Now don't misunderstand me. I'm not advocating that everyone start
going to horse races and betting their motorhome gas money. I mean
only to point out that we drag our feet when we get opportunities to
try new things. I wonder how many of us take advantage of the myriad
opportunities for wonderful experiences that we motorhomers are
exposed to in our travels? How many times do we zip right past signs
that point the way to historical or geological or cultural "little gems" on

our way to "big diamonds"? How often we opt not to try something simply because it might not be all that interesting or it is out of our way? The same applies for involvement with people. Sometimes we pass up chances to participate in people-functions that could lead to new friendships and exciting activities. Why? Because it's easier to do nothing than it is to try something new. Inertia! As the physicist defines it—a body at rest tends to stay at rest. Or, put more bluntly, we act like old poops.

Nature, of course, slows people down physically as they get older. That is a simple fact that most of us accept. However, that doesn't mean that we should just roll over and start dying. In fact, lots of folks fight back; they resist the tendency to stay at rest. We frequently see wonderful examples of physical feats among men and women long past the ages normally associated with physical accomplishments. The other day, I saw a picture and story about a woman diver and swimmer working out regularly at age ninety-two! She's a shining example of how some people meet physical challenges in spite of their years. It's a way to keep young in the body.

Similarly, some older folks meet mental challenges in spite of their years. As inertia affects the physical side of us, so it affects the mental side. Very simply, brains that not regularly exercised tend to stay at rest. We need constantly to keep our heads stirred up. That's why we should always be ready and willing to try new things. Whether it's new people, new places, or new things, we should be very reluctant to say, "I'm too old for that." Rather, when an opportunity arises to try something new—and we should always be alert to those opportunities—our response should be, "I'll try it."

Incidentally, I'm going to the races again tomorrow. I figure if I double my bets, I'll make $56.

■ ■ ■

February 1995

Reunions

L arge families are fortunate. I know. I'm from one. Growing up with enough siblings to field a full baseball team (four broth- ers and the same number of sisters) was a wonderful time, in spite of the difficulties we, as most families we knew, endured in obtain- ing life's basic necessities during the Great Depression. The nine Maxwell kids were usually too busy having fun to dwell on their state of poverty.

But that was a long time ago. When those "kids" get together now, the games they play are different. The whooping and hollering and run- ning have been replaced with sitting under the maples and discussing grandkids, ailments, and Medicare.

We were outdoor kids. Summer or winter, we savored what Mother Nature offered us. As country kids, we had the woods, the ponds, the creeks, and the fields. Whether it was swimming, fishing, hunting, or just playing, we were outdoors most of the time.

Credit that love of the outdoors when we were young with the fact that several of the Maxwell kids made camping important in their own families' lives. Of course that camping eventually became RVing, as that industry became more popular and the clan became more affluent. Most of us have owned camping rigs of some type, and presently three of us are motorhomers.

Last August, we had a family reunion at the old homesite in Illi- nois. The house we grew up in is long gone and has been replaced with an easy-to-maintain mobile home. But Mom is still there, and as long as she is, it will be home.

All nine of Mom's kids were there together for the first time in almost a decade. Although she's remarkably spry mentally, almost nine decades of some very hard years have taken their toll physically. She fends for herself most of the time, but she's definitely not able to cook and care for nine kids (ages fifty to seventy). Add to that number the spouses and some grandkids, and there was a whole passel of us.

Some had to find sanctuary with other relatives because of space limitations in the mobile home, but the three of us with motorhomes pulled our rigs into RV spaces beside the garden. Full hookups, no less— thanks to the Mr. Fix-it brother who lives near Mom. From the comfort of our own homes, we enjoyed a grand get-together. Yet we still had our own privacy when we wanted it.

I have long maintained that the best way to visit friends and relatives is in your RV. It's a way to enjoy a visit without creating extra work for your hosts. It's also a way to avoid the inconvenience of having to pack and unpack clothes and the discomfort of sleeping on beds that don't feel like your own. It's a way to have your toothbrush in your own rack. Even the finest hotel can't provide the one special thing that your RV can when you are away from home and that is a feeling of home. It's wonderful to visit friends and relatives, but no matter how much you love them, it is difficult to share twenty-four hours a day with them. Each of us functions in a unique way with different interests, ideas, and ways of doing things. We simply get on each other's nerves if we are edged off our private tracks. Your own motorhome in someone's driveway assures you of a way to keep on your track.

The reunion has been over for some time now. We have pictures of all nine kids with Mom, and there are shots of the spouses and grandkids. Best of all, we have memories. New pages have been added to the family's history. It's getting to be a mighty thick book now.

Thanks, Mom, for giving me so many brothers and sisters.

■ ■ ■

Time to Spare

Margie and I travel some 25,000 miles per year doing our seminar program. That means a lot of hours on the road, often on interstates that we have traveled many times before. Unfortunately, some of the scenery isn't exactly exciting, for example, that stretch on Interstate 10 between Fort Stockton and El Paso.

As the full-time driver of our rig, I'm forced to look out the windshield at all times. Fortunately, whether it is desert or mountains or plains or seashore, I almost always find something that is interesting to see. And, of course, there's always the need to keep an eye on traffic, front and rear.

Passengers don't have the requirement to watch where drivers are going, so they have time to spare. One way to occupy that time is to help the pilot with specific driving instructions, particularly those pertaining to speed or closeness to the car ahead. And every motorhome driver with a nervous copilot has heard, "Oh, oh, watch it; you're too close to the edge," when you are traveling on mountain roads. However, most passengers look for other ways to kill time as they travel through unexciting territory.

Margie is an avid reader and spends many hours with her books. In fact, when she gets a really engrossing one, she forgets what is happening and doesn't even help me with those important driving instructions. Fortunately, she usually feels like helping when we're on a road with a drop-off on her side (I don't drive on roads with cliffs on my side) and helps me through the tight spots.

Naps are a way of passing time for Margie. Every day that we're on the road, she takes a couple of snoozes. In fact, it isn't uncommon for her to sleep all the way from Fort Stockton to El Paso. I envy her at times. Believe me, that is pretty dull country.

It's a good thing the road is wide and straight, because I don't get any help from her for several hours. But, again I somehow muddle through.

Margie used to knit. As a matter of fact, she has made several beautiful afghans while on the road. She gave them all away. I'm rather glad she gave up that time-passer because I got tired of tripping on that yarn bag all the time. Besides, she promised me one of the afghans to drape around my shoulders on cool evenings, but she always gave them away to more important people, like kids and grandkids.

I'd say that the best time-passer is when we take grandkids, but they have a tendency to be bored unless there's something really spectacular going on—like a volcano erupting or a jet plane crashing. That's when we bring out all the games, both old and new, such as Monopoly, Trivial Pursuit, and all types of hand-held computer-driven sports games. Popcorn and sodas make it a real party. I hear them laughing and know they're enjoying the RVing.

Recently, we got a new way to pass the hours that puts all other methods to shame. It has gripped Margie's attention like no highway spectacle ever has. In fact, she has almost forsaken me at the wheel and lets me drive without any help.

What is this new, magic timekiller? A little hand-held, computer-driven poker machine! For someone who has a penchant for the whirling wheels at Las Vegas, it is a marvelous invention. Margie has that whirling-wheel penchant, so ever since I got her the machine last summer, she has kept it with her like a kid with a security blanket. I can't really say that it has replaced Las Vegas as an outlet for the gambling urge, but it has certainly proved to be one of the greatest time-killers ever invented.

She loves it—and so do I!

■ ■ ■

April 1995

It's Not All Troubles

First impressions are so important. How often a decision hinges on what a person perceives when he or she sees something for the first time, for example, how many marriages have resulted from the whammo effect that sometimes occurs when boys and girls first see each other. It makes me wonder at times how many prospective motorhomers are turned away from the RV lifestyle by the impressions they get from reading about motorhome troubles in RV publications.

For the benefit of readers who conclude from reading the "RV troubles" columns that motorhomers devote most of their time to fixing their machines, let me tell you that you are mistaken. True, a lot of column space is devoted to problems, but that no more indicates that motorhoming is mostly fixing than it is to conclude from reading or hearing the daily news that living in America is mostly murdering, robbing, and raping. The reality is that most people don't commit crimes, nor are they crime victims. And, most motorhomers spend most of their time enjoying their machines rather than fixing them. What we have here is an example of the "creaking wheel" getting the major attention and, hopefully, some grease.

Admittedly and unfortunately, motorhomes do break. It's the nature of the beast. In fact, it is remarkable that so few problems stem from bouncing our houses around on the highways at 65 miles an hour. However, any break means problems and problem solving is what all those "troubles columns" are about. If John Geraghty, Brian Robertson, and the other technical writers can solve the machinery problems that go with the RV lifestyle, then most of the rest is smooth sailing. But smooth-sailing stories, like ordinary happy-life stories, don't make the papers like stories about bad things.

Margie and I have been RVing for a very long time. We've had our share of problems—mechanical, weather, and those caused by people. Some have been very severe (burning up a new motorhome), and others have been very troublesome (transmission going out), but most have been far less serious. We've certainly spent our share of time in repair shops and suffered the bewilderment that comes with trying to cope with broken things while on the road.

But if I look at the overall time span that we've been RVing and compare the problem times with the good times, it's no contest. The latter probably accounts for 95 percent of our time in motorhomes. However, the remaining 5 percent has gotten far more than that percentage of our attention.

For example, burning up that motorhome has consumed more of our time in discussions than talk about the miles and miles of bluebonnets that line Interstate 10 in Texas in the spring. We've spent a lot more time seeing things that were beautiful and doing interesting things than we have suffering disasters, but the latter gets an undue amount of attention.

So, the point I wish to convey to novices is this: Don't be too quick to conclude that taking up motorhoming is an open invitation to troubles.

We have them, sure, and in spite of the fact that motorhomes get better all the time and the tech people keep solving problems, I'm sure that some troubles will plague every motorhomer. Being willing to deal with those problems is simply a part of the game. However, as any experienced motorhomer will tell you, the good times far outweigh the bad. Just ask any of them to tell you about their favorite campsites, their favorite places, their favorite trips, and their best times.

■ ■ ■

May 1995

Ph.D. in RVing?

I f colleges granted advanced degrees for general education, I'd know a lot of masters and doctors. It has been my observation that there is a direct relationship between knowing and traveling. As I frequently say in my seminars, "Show me a longtime RVer, and I'll show you a well-educated person." The fact is that the kinds of people who are attracted to the lifestyle are usually curious, eager, and active.

There's something about seeing it, feeling it, being in it, that makes our travel experiences more meaningful than reading about places in books or seeing them on television. Let's take a look at some examples of what I mean.

Probably history ranks as Number 1 in courses of study for which RVers sign up. Witness the number of motorhomes you see at parks and monuments devoted to famous events in our past. Gettysburg, for example. Plenty of good RV parks in the area suggest the popularity of that destination for RVers. It is one of those places where you get to feel as well as see history. If you go through the audiovisual offerings first and read some of the literature provided, you will probably enjoy and understand the actual tour of the battlefield better. It would be difficult for a person to spend a full day (better yet, two) at Gettysburg and not have a good comprehension of that famous turning point in our history.

How about those geography lessons you get as you tour the various regions of the United States? I feel sorry for people who have only read about the saguaro forests of southern Arizona; or for those who have never experienced the top-of-the-world feeling you get as you crest an 11,000-foot pass in Colorado; or savored the feeling of grandeur that comes with viewing the incredible rock formations in Arches National

Park, Utah; or watched and heard the breakers at Montauk Point, New York. The list of wonderful places is endless, but the avid RVer keeps looking and learning.

Besides seeing places, RVers see how people vary in their ways of living. Those who have visited the Pueblo at Taos, New Mexico, as well as the Amish farms in Lancaster, Pennsylvania, recognize that America means many different cultures: a dose of sociology along with history and geography.

Travelers who stray from the main highways to Dinosaur National Monument, Colorado, get a glimpse of the paleontologists' discipline. How remarkable to see our prehistory revealed by their patient labors.

The scientific mind gets abundant opportunity to expand in visits to the many museums and exhibits available to the RV traveler. For example, those intrigued by space travel should visit NASA facilities at Houston, Texas; Huntsville, Alabama; and Cape Kennedy, Florida.

For those more inclined toward the arts, how about the lessons you learn when visiting some of the hundreds of wonderful art museums around the country? There's something for every taste—like the John Ringling home in Sarasota, Florida, to the Remingtons at the Cowboy Hall of Fame, Oklahoma City, Oklahoma (both prime examples of museums easily accessible to the motorhomer in his rig).

Of course, RVing students of nature have opportunities everywhere and of every kind to satisfy their thirst for knowledge. Our great parks, national, state, and local, offer a fabulous wealth of flora and fauna ranging from the cypress islands and 'gators of the Everglades to the lichens and grizzly bears of Alaska.

The USA is a wonderful schoolroom, and RVers are among its best students.

■ ■ ■

June 1995

Holding Hands

A sight that creates a pleasant, lighthearted feeling in me is a lithe, exuberant, obviously love-struck young boy and girl holding hands. That feeling is even more pronounced when I see a whiteheaded, timeworn, but very contented-looking, couple strolling hand-in-hand. Fortunately, it is a sight that I am quite regularly treated to in campgrounds and RV parks.

In my seminars on fulltiming (as well as in my book on that subject), I emphasize one of the unique circumstances in which RVing couples find themselves, particularly fulltimers. Twenty-four hours a day, seven days a week, thirty or thirty-one days a month, they are within shouting distance of each other—frequently within striking distance. The point is this: RV couples must like each other. And it's even better if that like is accompanied by a big dose of love. Which brings us to hand-holding—one of the more common displays of liking and loving.

I guess I'm sentimental about hand-holding because Margie and I have been great handholders for more than half a century (forty-five of those years married). Apparently, we meet the necessary levels of like and love criteria, considering the years we've spent in RVs and we're still hand-holding. And, obviously, we're in plenty of like-company because, as we take our frequent strolls, it is an unusual day that we don't meet other hand-holding couples who are our age.

It's my unscientifically proven belief that there's more hand-holding among RVers than among "regular people." Maybe this phenomenon is due to the kind of people who are attracted to the lifestyle, or maybe it's that the lifestyle creates the urge to hand-hold. Anyway, I'm pleased to be in such good company—which brings me to a point.

Since I'm not a columnist for the lovelorn, nor do I profess to be an expert on marital relations, I won't presume to give any expert advice on how to gild the Golden Years.

Since RVers have so many options about when, where, and what they do, they should regularly discuss and agree to a course of action. The fact that this is a problem is fresh in my memory. Just a couple of nights ago at a campground in Arizona, I casually asked my next-space neighbor how her winter was going. Boy, oh, boy, did she start letting off steam. Her complaint was that she had just been dragged by a thoughtless husband through thousands of miles over a period of months from one fishing hole to another. She was completely fed up with being where she did not want to be—doing what she didn't want to be doing. Accordingly, they were on the way back to Oregon.

Another area in which we men, particularly, are apt to be a bit unreasonable is in the distribution of labor as we travel. More often than not, men do most of the driving and handling of maintenance problems. Some of us let our chore list stop with those things while we expect our companions to do everything else. And that just isn't fair. Driving a motorhome several hundred miles in a day is tiring, but so is riding. The man who plops in his chair after hooking up for the night, flips on the television, and expects his mate to cook a big dinner, wash the dishes, clean up the kitchen, do laundry, etc., before she gets to sit down is not demonstrating a very caring attitude.

My strongest recommendation for the creation of harmonious and happy travel is for both members of Golden Age couples to recall and reenact regularly the little things that set them a-tinglin' when they were young and first in love—like holding hands.

■ ■ ■

Are You Carrying?

To borrow a question from the gun-toters of the Old West and the gangsters of more modern times, how many of you carry a firearm in your motorhome? If you do, are you aware of the possible consequences if you use it to protect yourself from a threat to your person or property? By displaying the weapon, you may be in violation of a gun law. You may end up being arrested along with the criminal you were protecting yourself from!

My intent here is not to take a position as a pro-gun or anti-gun advocate. It is simply to point out the reality that those who take certain types of guns in their RVs are in some places in violation of gun laws.

For example, after a column on guns several years ago, I was contacted by a lady who was desperately trying to get a felony conviction overturned. It meant an eight-year sentence for the possession of an illegal weapon (a revolver) in a vehicle. I couldn't help her. Very simply, she had violated the law in the state where her motorhome was searched and the weapon found. She went to trial. Her defense was that her motorhome was her home and that she had a right to have the weapon in her home. That defense didn't work. The jury brought in a verdict of guilty. And that is the verdict that would be reached in many instances where RVers are found to be "carrying an illegal weapon in a vehicle."

Of course, today's many gun laws are bad news for RVers who like to "carry." But the good news is that there is a simple solution to this apparent dilemma. One can carry a gun and still not be in violation of most gun laws. The answer is a shotgun or a rifle. It's the short-barrel length that creates the legal problems, so rifles and shotguns don't violate laws.

It seems logical that if you feel the need to carry a gun, why not meet that need legally?

I recommend the pump shotgun. It can be a deterrent to a threat in two ways: (1) Just work the slide mechanism within hearing distance of the bad guy, and I guarantee you that in every case that metallic clack-clack will induce the sudden, very rapid departure of the criminal. (2) If you must shoot at someone in the dark, you can hit better with the shotgun. (Incidentally, it should be pointed out that if you shoot you'll probably be in violation of a law.)

And so the carrying problem is a complicated one. It seems that if you don't try to protect yourself from the robbers, murderers, rapists, thieves, etc., you are at their mercy; on the other hand, if you try to protect yourself from those criminals, you get in trouble with the law. But that's the way it is. Although I have no answer to the paradox, I think everyone who considers taking a gun should be aware of the possible consequences.

Crossing one of our borders, either to the north or the south, with a weapon is another matter. Canada is very strict about guns. Handguns are forbidden—period. Hunting guns can be taken in legally by following certain rules, which one can obtain from Canadian officials. Mexico is another matter. Their laws are very different from ours. Very simply, if you do take a gun and the police for some reason discover it, you may or may not have a problem. But if it is the former, the problem may be almost insurmountable. In short, taking a gun into Mexico is risky business.

In my seminars, I discuss the gun question, but I don't get much feedback. The problem is that many men don't want to air their gun feelings in public. But I would like very much to know those feelings. I particularly want to hear about legal problems stemming from "carrying."

■ ■ ■

Good Ol' Days

A recent letter from a reader lamented the passing of the good ol' days when RVing was a simple, gypsy way to retire, a time, when it got dark, we parked in any likely spot, prices were cheaper, and people were friendlier. He contrasted those days with these times when he considers RVs, RV parks, supply stores, and repair facilities to cater to the unfriendly, snobbish, and well-heeled.

That letter made me reflect on the more than three decades that we've been RVing, to see if I've missed something. I agree with some of his observations, but with reservations. However, I think I understand most of the economic changes he noted and don't find them particularly unusual in terms of the times. The fact is that there are logical explanations for most of the increases in costs connected with RVing.

The only fair way to measure the increased cost of RVing is to compare it with increases in the prices of other products and services. If we do that, we must note that in the mid-1970s, even after the huge increases in the cost of gasoline after the first energy crisis, we were still paying less than half of what we're paying now. Remember when we first talked about dollar-a-gallon gasoline? As for campground fees, many private RV parks charged less than $10 a night; indeed, many were almost half that. Labor rates at many RV repair shops were well under $20 an hour. And as for RVs themselves, wow! The typical Class C motorhome sold for well under $20,000 in 1975; some midsize Class As were available for little more.

But have RVs and RVing costs really increased out of proportion to the rest of the economy? I won't belabor you with a bunch of figures to prove my point, but, as we all know, everything has gone up. Try to think of something that doesn't cost several times more today than it did twenty years ago. Just compare the value of your house (if you have one) in 1975 with its value today. As for income, most working people are paid considerably more today than they were twenty years ago. Of course, I am aware that not all increases were proportionate to increased costs of living, but, overall, people take home more dollars today than they did then.

So, in general, I have to agree that RVing costs are up, but those increases are due simply to the changes in our economy. However, the increase in the quality and number of RV products and services is a factor that makes RVing more expensive today than two decades ago. Most obvious are motorhomes themselves. Compare a typical mid-'70s model with a new '95. New rigs are better looking, made of better materials, have more features and more options, and give better performance than their predecessors.

When it comes to campgrounds and RV parks, we're in a different ball game than we were twenty years ago. At that time, the amenities that we take for granted today were just beginning to be used. Luxury parks, as we know them now, were far and few between. One of the principal reasons for price increases in RVing is that we want better places to park our rigs. The marketplace has simply responded with better, more expensive places.

As for increases in labor rates at repair shops, I can only say that just as cars have become increasingly more complicated, so have RVs. Both demand bigger and better-equipped facilities with bigger and better-trained staffs—and increased costs to operate, which get passed on to customers.

But as for the friendliness of today's RVer compared with yesterday's, I have to disagree with my reader. RVers are still by far the friendliest bunch of people you could ever meet.

■ ■ ■

January 1996

More on "Carrying"

A few months ago, I addressed the issue of carrying guns in an RV. I pointed out that as much as we would like to, we do not have simple answers to questions that law-abiding RVers ask. There can be serious problems emanating from being caught "carrying" and the decision to carry or not deserves special attention. Since this is such a contradictory issue, I asked readers for their input. And I got it!

I was pleased to discover that most letters indicated general approval of my recommendation that, if you feel the necessity to carry, a pump shotgun should be the weapon of choice. Because of the increasing number of handgun laws, that course of action seem logical to me. I was also pleased to read the many suggestions that were given regarding the loading and use of the shotgun. Although it is impossible to cite and summarize all the information I received, I'll pass on some of the suggestions.

Several people pointed out the most fundamental questions that anyone who proposes to carry a gun should ask themselves: Could I really shoot a human being? Could I bear the guilt feelings that might come with killing someone? If the answer is "no" to either of these questions, then you shouldn't carry a gun!

I received the following suggestions from you readers:

- Although, theoretically, the Constitution stipulates that "Full Faith and Credit shall be given in each State to the public Acts, Records, and judicial proceedings of every other State," don't count on that clause to include gun laws.
- If you choose to carry a shotgun, then consider firing a tear-gas or rock-salt load as your first shot.

- Carrying an unloaded gun is less likely to create a law violation.
- Do not consider the answers and advice from a policeman you know as being valid in other jurisdictions.
- There is general agreement that "I would rather be tried by twelve than carried by six."
- Finally, don't ask and don't tell.

A number of letters requested information regarding gun laws because the writers are interstate travelers, and they don't want to get into trouble by carrying guns. Many have attempted to get a clarification from various agencies, but no one has entirely succeeded. A lack of consistency among states' laws makes the waters murky. Even some police departments are unable to properly advise citizens of their jurisdictions.

A part of the problem is that laws are constantly changing; another is that there are differing interpretations of existing laws. For example, it is not legally clear whether or not a motorhome is a home, even if you live in it full time and are thereby subject to the same legal protections as a house. To all of you who are looking for answers to the question of whether or not to carry, I'm sorry to say that those answers aren't available. I don't want to be in the position of giving legal advice. I am not a lawyer and, besides, I doubt if many lawyers fully understand the issue of carrying a gun in a motorhome.

However, I'm not giving up. Presently I am writing to the attorney general of each state to request the most current information. Unfortunately, my requests will not be given red-carpet treatment, I'm sure, so it will be some time before I have the information to digest. When I do get it, I will pass along what I learn.

Meantime, anyone who prowls around my motorhome late at night might hear the "clack-clack" sound of the pump action of my 20-gauge. You see, I, too, "would rather be tried by twelve than carried by six."

■ ■ ■

July 1996

Something Old,
Something New

The greatest stumbling block to discovering new ways of enjoying motorhoming is inertia coupled with fear. We develop habits that are comfortable and satisfying so we tend to deviate from them only reluctantly. Why, we ask ourselves, should we take the risk of not enjoying something when we are satisfied with what we've been doing? In short, we get into a comfortable rut and keep repeating the same things—the same routes, the same parks/campgrounds, the same areas, the same activities, the same goals, and the same people.

Many people fear change, particularly as they get older. If we already know a route to some place—the roads are good, the traffic is not too bad, there are no dangerous sections, etc.—we feel safe with that knowledge. But if we try a new route, there's no telling what we might encounter, we consciously or unconsciously tell ourselves. So we keep going the same old way.

Many RVers never venture away from the same campgrounds. Some go to the same one time after time, year after year. They know what those places are like, and they are uncomfortable with the idea of going to some unfamiliar place. (The spaces might be too tight, the ground not level, the bathrooms dirty, the clubhouse too small, the people unfriendly—lots of scary possibilities!)

And the same kind of thinking applies to people. Not uncommonly some folks limit themselves to a small circle of friends and make little effort to involve new people in their lives. Again, the fear of the unknown.

Most of those fears are unfounded. After all, when you consider the reasons why we are motorhomers, isn't it because we are adventurous, curious, and interested in seeing and doing new things?

Every time we decide against turning down that different road, or stopping at that new place, or meeting new people, aren't we defeating the purpose for our lifestyle? Conversely, just think of the pleasures we have had in discovering new places, people, and things because we ventured into the new and unknown. Of course, not everything new and different is wonderful, but being willing to accept some of the bad is the only way we'll discover some of the good things that come from motorhoming.

I'm sure that all of us started out motorhoming with a sense of excitement Perhaps we need to occasionally look back to the day we got in that new motorhome for the first time and drove it home: the elation we felt as we pulled out onto the highway from the dealer's lot; how proud we felt as we pulled into the driveway at home; the exciting planning that went into that first trip. Then, the joy that came with the discovery that travel in a motorhome provides a degree of comfort that makes travel by car/motel/restaurants or by air, primitive indeed. And all of it while traveling new roads and discovering new places, people, and things. We need to recall those feelings every once in a while to remind us of what motorhoming is all about.

To help you revive those feelings, I have a suggestion. Plan your next trip to do something you've never done before. Select a destination that you know about because you either heard about it from someone else or read about it or you simply passed the sign that pointed to it. You have wanted to see it but for various reasons never made it. Perhaps it's a ghost town in the desert, a national park, an old town, or historical site. Then plan your trip to it over roads that you've never been on—go for the red (or blue) lines; heck, even tackle some of the grays. Better yet, if you really feel brave, try some of the other roads, the ones that are narrow double lines on maps.

One of the most memorable of our wanderings was the time we took off from Willcox, Arizona, headed for Tombstone via other roads. We stirred up a lot of road dust and did considerable shaking and bouncing, but we discovered the remains of two ghost towns, Pearce and Gleeson, where we spent the night at an unnamed campground for two trucks. Plus, I got a personally narrated tour of a real gold mine by the only human we saw there (Margie doesn't like to go into big holes in the ground). I don't recall his name, but I do remember he was friendly and interesting. That was more than fifteen years ago, but it is a treasured memory that I will never forget. All because we dared to let our Daniel Boone genes take the lead.

We've been parked in the same spot for more than a month, but we're headed out in a few days. I know what our ultimate destination is, but on the way, I think I'll just turn off on a side road somewhere so that we may see something we've never seen before.

Maybe this is a case of the doctor taking his own medicine.

■ ■ ■

August 1996

First RV Trip

C an you remember the details of your first RV trip? I'll bet you can. In fact, you're probably like me. So many things went awry that it's a wonder there was a second trip. But, like all real campers, we just took the bad with the good and chalked it all up to experience.

Our first trip wasn't in a motorhome. In 1954, they didn't have such things. But we had seen camping trailers and suspected that they were more appropriate for our needs than a tent. So we arranged to rent a 14-footer for our first-ever vacation. Thus began a week that could comprise a modern *Comedy of Errors.*

The mistakes began with our packing. Little did we imagine the effects of the bouncing and swaying that takes place in a little trailer being dragged down the highway. But we sure learned at our first gas stop when we opened the trailer to check on things. The floor was a garbage bucket—sugar, flour, ketchup, broken eggs, broken bottles, and dented cans, all floating in soda pop and beer. Our education in how to pack began at that moment with fundamentals like putting the pin in the icebox door and using containers that don't spill easily. We cleaned up and went on.

Mistake number two was leaving for Yosemite in the late afternoon. But when you're under thirty and rarin' to go, you don't do everything logically, even with two little ones. We began to wonder at the wisdom of our departure time, however, when we blew a muffler at midnight. Fortunately, the kids slept through the installation of a new one at an all-night service station.

The next goof was the place we selected in the dark to pull off for a few hours' sleep. Campgrounds along the highways were indeed rarities in those days, so you took advantage of whatever open spaces became available. The spot we picked by the light of our headlights appeared to be plenty wide, so we settled in for the night. Suddenly, we were violently awakened by a screaming, roaring, shuddering blast. We had parked about twenty feet from a railroad and Old 99 was making good time up through the San Joaquin Valley It was followed by Old 88 and a few others, so sleep was quite broken, to say the least.

The next day we arrived at our destination—beautiful Yosemite National Park. In those days, one camped on the valley floor (Camp Curry) among the trees with campfires and the whole outdoor bit. I don't recall what all we did that first day, but I remember vividly the first night. In those days, with those small trailers, creating sleeping spaces required some ingenuity. One of those spaces was a small overhead bunk where we "logically" placed our four-year-old daughter. Unfortunately, in the middle of the night, she rolled out of bed for a five-foot drop to the floor on her nose. We spent the next couple of hours trying to console her as we berated ourselves for our stupidity in putting her in that bunk without adequate safety precautions.

The next day brought no problems with the trailer, but, unfortunately, a serious accident for our two-year-old son. Our breakfast was simmering on a perfect bed of coals when our bouncy boy backed up and fell into the coals on his bottom. Although we immediately came to his aid, he had put his hands down to push himself up and burned his wrists quite badly. Margie is an RN, so she treated the wounds. But we again spent hours trying to console a child as we again castigated ourselves for not preventing the accident.

After a few days at Yosemite, we hitched up and took off for San Francisco to visit relatives. Mistake number umpteen: Too much ground covered in too little time. But when you are young, very busy, and poor, you try to do everything. We made that mistake more than once—even when we got older.

I daresay that most RVers have made the "open-window" mistake. We did it, too. When we stopped for the day, we found out what happens when you leave trailer windows open on a dusty road. It took an hour or so to make the place habitable. But, the good news: we learned a lesson. After that, we made a window check every time we hitched up.

Our final mistake came upon returning home at the end of the week with the rented trailer. We knew our return date was such and such, but we didn't note the time it was due back. We got in too late to return it that day. Rushing it in the next morning did not fulfill the contract. We had forfeited our deposit—something we could ill afford in those days.

Mistakes, yes; dampened enthusiasm for camping, no! It's forty-two years later and we're still very, very happy campers.

■ ■ ■

September 1996

Reverse Snowbirds

T raditionally the northern RV snowbird flies south for the winter. In late autumn, he flees from the coming snow and ice that will soon envelop his old homestead to the warm climes of the Sunbelt. And when the daffodils bloom and the sap runs in April, he returns to a normal lifestyle up north.

And so it was for many years until a new and fast-growing trend developed that has reversed the order of things. Now, many snowbirds have opted for maintaining a home base in the Sunbelt and traveling north in the summer. It is a phenomenon that is not likely to lose momentum.

Why this big change? As long-time RV snowbird friends of ours reported to us last winter, they discovered that their priorities in friends and activities have gradually shifted from their traditional lifestyle in Spokane, Washington, to their RV lifestyle in Yuma, Arizona. Along with that shift in priorities, they found that their eagerness to be in the south changed their pattern from leaving home in fall and returning in spring to just the opposite. Also, they found a corresponding change in the use of various services connected with daily living. They began to rely more on medical services, automotive repairs, hair care, etc., near their winter home. And they became more involved socially with their winter friends. In fact, they found that in the summer, they focused more on visits from and visits to winter friends than they did their old friends. With that change in priorities, it seemed logical to establish their main residence in Yuma and use their motorhome for summer travel in cooler places.

In terms of economics, that big shift can be very beneficial to the bank account. Although traditional snowbirds who have kept their houses may leave home for four to six months, the bills for utilities, taxes, insurance, and maintenance go on for twelve. Maintaining a home is expensive. So, by selling the old homestead, one can usually acquire the funds to establish a smaller home in the south and have money left over.

Most of the reverse snowbirds choose the park-model trailer for their permanent home in their winter roost. That type of rig, although legally defined as an RV, is definitely not a vehicle in the usual sense. Actually, they are trailers that are pulled on the highway only two times— first from the manufacturer to the dealer and the second time from the dealer to the site where the consumer wants it set up. And there it stays, set up permanently like a mobile home.

Park models are limited legally to under 400 square feet, so, consequently most are 399 square feet in floor space. Often, owners add 400-square-foot Florida rooms (in Arizona, Arizona rooms) to give a total of 800 square feet of living space. Certainly an adequate amount of living space for a couple of empty-nesters who want to scale down the amount of work normally required to maintain a house. Placed in an RV park where lots are small and yard work minimal, it leaves the residents free for fun and games.

Compared with the price of houses, park models are quite inexpensive. They range in price from $15,000 to double that amount. Usually, they are fully furnished. Set up with an added room in a rental park, the total cost of a nice 800-square-foot home normally runs around $30,000 to $40,000. Of course, many people opt to buy lots in condo parks, which can add anywhere from $8,000 to as high as $50,000-plus (in luxury resorts) to the total cost of a park-model home.

One might ask: Why not choose a much larger mobile home rather than a park model if you are going to settle down somewhere? The answer is simply that mobile homes go in mobile home parks and park models go in RV parks. That means two different lifestyles, and RVers, generally, are more suited for the latter.

Most motorhomers who opt for the park model home base in the south keep their motorhomes for summer travel. It gives them a chance to visit their families and old haunts, as well as the freedom to see some of the places they have passed up in previous summers because of the necessity to be at home for the myriad chores that living in a house requires. Most find it a tremendous release from the worry and constraints of regular home ownership. Incidentally, since they are usually located behind gates in RV parks, park model owners have few worries about their places when they leave for months at a time.

I'm not suggesting that all motorhome owners who still own homes rush to put their houses on the market so they can establish new park-model residences in the south. But I do know that most of us at some time find the house burdensome. For the avid snowbird, that's the time to explore the park model avenue. And, possibly become a reverse snowbird.

■ ■ ■

January 1997

Snowbird Roosts: Arizona

H ollywood typically portrays the deserts of Arizona as the suburbs of hell. Summer travelers through Gila Bend will certainly not dispute that view. When the temperature hovers in the 110°F to 120°F range, few northerners will concede that such places are habitable. Yet many of those same people—as RV snowbirds—flock to those same deserts as the winter chill descends on their homelands and summer's hell becomes winter's paradise.

Long before the advent of the RV, well-to-do folks had discovered that the winter ambiance of Scottsdale and Tucson was far superior to that of Detroit and Chicago. Fortunately, for those of us with shallower pockets, the RV lifestyle permits us to enjoy those balmy climes, too. The result is a flooding of the many popular snowbird roosts by flocks of RVers every autumn.

Even with continuous park development, present Phoenix-area facilities are usually bursting at the seams in January and February. New parks, many of which are elegant resorts with wonderful amenities— clubhouses with huge dance floors, arts-and-crafts workshops, pools and spas, pool rooms, exercise rooms, tennis courts, even golf courses— supervised by social directors, appear to be trying to outdo each other in services for their tenants or owners. Of course, some of the new parks emphasize good basic facilities with moderate costs.

Probably the Phoenix area is the oldest—certainly the most popular—RV snowbird choice. Actually, most of the parks are in the Mesa area; however, development has pushed eastward through Apache Junction, where new parks are proliferating. Venture Out, the granddaddy of condominium resorts, was built in Mesa in the early 1970s. Many others followed, along with scores of rental parks, both large and small.

However, not all of the Phoenix-area parks are in Mesa. To the northwest are several large, nice ones, and there are a few directly north. All are within reasonable distances of good shopping areas. Prospective Phoenix-area snowbirds would be wise to stop at a park for a short stay while they scout the entire area before they commit to a long-term rental contract or purchase a lot.

RVers who are looking for winter roosts with a more urban atmosphere—plenty of restaurants, mall shopping, golf, and other good city stuff—should definitely consider the Phoenix area. However, they should also be prepared for some of the bad city stuff, like horrendous smog, crime, and lots of people.

Yuma has become a snowbird haven for a population that exceeds that of its year-round residents. Its initial attraction, besides a winter climate that is possibly the best in Arizona, was its bargain prices, especially in park spaces and restaurants.

Until the mid-1980s, there were no large, fancy resort-type parks. However, that has changed, and Yuma now has a broad spectrum that accommodates almost any amenity requirements or pocketbooks. Although Yuma still maintains a relatively small-town atmosphere, due to its size, its traffic at certain hours is almost citylike. Also, due to the local citrus industry, chemical spraying presents a problem to some people with respiratory problems. And, of course, people who like the sound of airplanes definitely should choose a park near the Marine Corps Air Station.

There's plenty to do in Yuma. Old Mexico is just a few miles away, and nearly every Yuma snowbird makes regular shopping trips to San Luis and/or Algodones. Several modestly priced golf courses are available to the public. Shopping facilities for essentials (food, clothing, restaurants, etc.) are adequate and relatively low-priced.

Tucson, although a beautiful city with a marvelous history, is not as popular as a snowbird roost as are Phoenix and Yuma, probably because the temperature generally runs several degrees cooler than the other two cities.

Boondocking has its greatest popularity in Arizona. Not only does it have the great winter climate, but it has enormous Bureau of Land Management (BLM) tracts that constitute the bulk of land available for boondocking. Quartzsite is the most popular such area and is growing rapidly. Thousands of RVers spend the entire winter out in the boonies where new services make that lifestyle relatively civilized. Although the BLM now charges a modest use fee, it provides dump stations, water stations, and trash collection. The Imperial Dam Area north of Yuma and Pilot Knob west of the city (both are in California) are the most popular boondock camps.

For additional information about and of these areas, call the chambers of commerce in the appropriate cities or the BLM in Yuma.

■ ■ ■

February 1997

RVers and Service Managers: Us Versus Them?

O ne of the basic realities—and frustrations—of motorhoming is that our machines break. Compounding the frustrations associated with the actual breakdowns are those encountered in getting repairs.

There seem to be some fixed rules about breakdowns. First, they usually occur on weekends, often the Saturday morning of a three-day weekend. Second, you're always at least fifty miles from the nearest service shop. Third, when you do finally get to that shop, you find that the service people are swamped with work and that it will be at least a day or more before they can get to you. Fourth, when someone finally looks at your problem, it is worse than you thought and hence will cost more to repair than you expected. And finally, the service manager (and everyone else at the dealership) doesn't seem to care about your problems. So the only logical thing to do is obvious: Blame the service manager.

Well, from our perspective (that is, the broken-down consumer), that may be the thing to do, but from the service manager's desk, it certainly isn't. So, for an exercise in role-switching, I'm going to look at the problem from his standpoint. After all, haven't we been told that we should not criticize someone unless we've walked in the other guy's shoes?

Actually, I've talked to some service managers about how they think they and their customers can best deal with each other in the most harmonious and beneficial ways. Invariably they claim that they are aware of and sympathize with their customers' problems and they always try their best to solve them. But, being defensive of their own positions, they point out that, all too often, customers precipitate problems with unrealistic expectations and demands when they come in for service.

As proof of how that happens, one manager cited these examples:

1. The customer who calls for an appointment to fix two things, but arrives with a list of seventeen items. Knowing that it takes an hour to fix two things, the service manager has scheduled a mechanic accordingly. Now he is faced with the question of what to do about the other fifteen items: cancel the other jobs that the mechanic was scheduled for and make the owners of those rigs unhappy, or make one unreasonable customer unhappy?

2. The impatient fellow who insists that his problems get taken care of first, regardless of other people's problems. He's the guy who hangs over the counter and complains about everything—how he paid a fortune for the rig to begin with and it has been nothing but trouble; how he got all kinds of promises of excellent after-sale service that aren't being kept; how much time he's spent in service shops, etc., etc.

3. The fellow who tries to get everything done under warranty, regardless of the problem. As an illustration, the service manager told me about a guy who wanted a new sofa to replace the one that "just came apart." Suspicions were aroused by what careful examination showed to be claw marks and the presence of a large Doberman reclining on the bed.

Although I have interviewed some service managers who seem to be unduly harsh in their views of customers, most aren't. In fact, the majority seem to be sympathetic with their customers' problems and do their best to alleviate them. Most feel that their customers are reasonable and understanding about the problems of running an efficient shop and are, consequently, reasonable in their requests. However, all claim that there are enough of those unreasonable types to make that other category of customer stand out.

As an avid, longtime motorhomer, I've spent my share (in fact, more than my share) of time in RV service shops. Since I'm not much of a Mr. Fix-it, I have to rely on those who are. If I were able to calculate the hours, days, weeks, or possibly even months that I've spent in repair shops over the past thirty-plus years, it would be an impressive amount of time. Yet, I don't despair. I try to put those hours to good use by talking with people, shopping, walking, or reading.

And I have learned to do my share of cooperating with service managers. First, if I make an appointment to get some things fixed, I stick to that list when I go in for the work. Second, although we would all like to think that our problems deserve special attention, they usually don't, so l don't expect service managers to put me at the top of the line just because my time is valuable. And, finally, we should not expect manufacturers and dealers to subsidize, through warranties, our carelessness or ignorance in caring for our equipment

I'm not saying that all service managers are wonderful and we RV customers are bums, but I am saying that we should picture ourselves in their shoes when we go in to get their help in keeping us on the road.

■ ■ ■

April 1997

What to Pack

One of the toughest jobs for RVers is to decide on what to pack when you are getting the motorhome ready for a trip. There's a variation on Murphy's Law that goes: "If there is a space in your motorhome, you will put something in it." And there's a corollary: "There's more to put in than there is place to put it."

It's bad enough when you're packing for a two-week vacation, but can you imagine what it is like if you are getting ready for fulltiming? Either way, there is a problem. Seldom is there enough space to take all you want to, so it boils down to deciding what you absolutely have to have and what is expendable. One thing for sure: Few motorhomers leave any space unfilled. The problem is in deciding just what to fill it with.

To complicate the problem, it isn't a one-man decision; it's almost invariably one man and one woman—and possibly a few kids who have their own needs. It isn't uncommon for a controversy to develop about who takes what. Therefore, there is a need for some rules to follow when packing, and the longer the trip is going to be, the more important it is to adhere to those rules.

I'm aware of the fact that no one can tell motorhomers in general what they should specifically take with them. We are too individualistic. What works for the couple or family involved with fishing probably won't work for those whose thing is square-dancing. What the machine-oriented man who does all his own maintenance and repairs takes along will be quite different from those who never get their hands greasy.

In terms of clothing, it's the same diversity The couple who spends most of their time involved with nature—fishing, rock-hounding, or hiking—may take outdoor-type clothing, whereas the couple who spends a lot of time attending social and cultural functions may need a supply of suits and dresses. But regardless of individual needs and preferences, every motorhome needs to be packed, and the problems of doing that have some basic similarities. Only the content varies.

Rule 1: Know what you are working with in terms of storage space. Look over every compartment, drawer, cabinet, and shelf carefully. Each party involved should know exactly how much space there is both inside and out, so you can be realistic about what can be packed and what can't. In some instances, especially with kids, assign certain spaces to certain people, and let them choose their own items to fit.

Rule 2: Make a list of everything you would like to take and assign priorities to each, based on need. Everyone needs clothes, but most of us don't need as much as we might take if we had unlimited space. In short, look at the space allotted for your clothes and select items that will fit in that space. If you have three feet of closet rod available, choose three feet of clothing, based on projections of what you know you will wear. Don't pack anything that doesn't fit you well or that you aren't sure you would wear. And don't take anything that you haven't worn in the last year.

Rule 3: Don't take extras of things that are replaceable on the road. Trying to take enough food for a three-week trip when you know that you will be near grocery stores regularly is wasting space. Ditto the machinery maintenance end of things. Taking a reasonable number of tools and repair equipment is mandatory; lugging around a case of oil and other assorted easily obtainable maintenance items is generally unnecessary.

Rule 4: Don't try to duplicate facilities and equipment that you have in a house. If you try to create a normal home kitchen with all the pots and pans, skillets, and various paraphernalia, you'll find that there isn't space to put it all. And the same with the machine-oriented man trying to create a 20 × 20-foot shop in the compartments of his motorhome. It won't work. Very simply, a 10-inch table saw won't fit in most motorhome compartments, and few women appreciate having it in the bedroom.

Rule 5: Especially if you are packing for full-time travel, each half of a couple should have veto power over what the other wants to take. You can talk about it, but sometimes it takes someone else's viewpoint for objectivity.

Rule 6: Reduce everything to its smallest size before packing. Some clothes can be packed tightly or rolled; pots and pans can be stacked together; some clothes can be arranged to take less space (for example, multiple-pants hangers can accommodate four pairs on one hanger). If you have a basement, usually packing things in boxes or trays utilizes space best. I like large plastic boxes with sturdy lids. They are stackable, and in a big basement you can easily store a dozen or more.

And, finally, *Rule 7*: Don't use every inch of space. Save some for the goodies you will purchase, find, pick up, or receive as gifts on your trip.

■ ■ ■

May 1997

Try a Club

No, I'm not writing an advice column on how to raise children. Nor am I suggesting a way to get the attention of dog owners who tarry in front of your space to let Rover answer nature's call. Rather, I am suggesting a way for neophyte motorhomers to get into the swing of life on wheels with the least amount of trial and tribulation and a maximum of good help and advice. In short, join an RV club.

Clubs come in all kinds and sizes. Some are huge and general, such as the nearly one-million-member Good Sam Club, which admits anyone with any kind of RV, Others are small and specific; the Cortez National Motorhome Club admits only owners of that brand of motorhome. Some limit memberships to one sex, as does RVing Women. Some are geared to people with a particular interest a church, a fraternal order, a hobby, or an occupation. Still others are organized to benefit a particular type of RVing, such as fulltiming.

There's no end to the list of special-interest clubs. However, the majority of such clubs are open only to the owners of particular brands of RVs: Holiday Rambler RV Club, Bounders United, Monaco International Club, etc. The new motorhome owner needs to explore all avenues and choose the one that best fits him or her.

Some clubs are national, even international, in scope, while others are limited to a small geographical area. However, national clubs generally are broken down into chapters that operate in limited areas. For example, very large associations, like the Good Sam Club, Family Motor Coach Association, and many of the brand-name clubs, are broken down into regional and local groups. Therefore, most participants in those

clubs are involved mainly at the local level, which means that most of
their RVing is done with a small group of people whom they get to know
quite well. RVers are generally gregarious by nature, and clubs offer an
opportunity to enjoy the camaraderie of fellow RVers, as well as the pleasures found in our great outdoors.

To some extent, RV clubs are training schools for novice RVers. Let a
new owner and his family appear at their first outing with a group of old
pros, and they'll find that most of them are willing—even eager—to share
the knowledge that they already have. All you have to do is ask for advice
or help, and it will be given. Nowhere will you find a group of people more
inclined to help their fellowman than RVers. Just let someone indicate
that he (or she) has a problem with his or her rig, and several Mr. Fix-
its will come to the rescue. Savor a new dish at a potluck, and you'll find
the cook ready and willing to share her recipe. See a new gadget or
modification on a rig, and be assured that the owner will gladly explain
its function, source, and cost. Seek advice on where to go and what to see,
and it will be forthcoming. In short, almost any RV club is a veritable
encyclopedia of information about RVs and the RV lifestyle.

For people who like to visit faraway places by RV, clubs can be a perfect avenue. Most of the larger clubs—and even some of the smaller
ones—offer both national and international caravans or group trips.
Popular tours include those to Alaska, Mexico, Canada, and Central
America. Tours within the contiguous United States usually focus on
special events, like the Mardi Gras in New Orleans, the Rose Parade in
Pasadena, and autumn in New England. Other popular tours visit special places, such as Branson, Missouri, and Nashville, Tennessee.

One of the greatest things about tours is that all the work and planning
are done for you by experts. For example, probably most RVers are apprehensive about making long trips to strange places, such as Mexico. They
don't know what to take, how to communicate, where to stay, how to cope

with problems, or what to see and do. That's where the tour planners earn their keep. Very simply, all you have to do is enjoy the scenery.

Another club benefit to its members—particularly to novices—is the formal education that often is part of club programs. At the national level, useful seminars on maintaining RVs or how best to enjoy the lifestyle are offered at major rallies. Also, club newsletters frequently deal with rig maintenance issues and new equipment and products.

To open a great avenue for learning about RVs and the enjoyment of RVing, try a club.

■ ■ ■

June 1997

Contrasts

L ast week Margie and I were parked in the middle of a desert, hooked up to a beaming sun, fresh air, a distant foreground of craggy mountains, and an incredible nightly display of stars. This week, we are at an elegant RV resort, replete with ballroom (Mel Tillis is playing Saturday), three swimming pools, spas, arts-and-crafts rooms, and a full-time professional activities director who keeps the place alive with planned events. The beaming sun is still with us, but our accommodations in these two places and what we do are a full 180 degrees apart. Yet, both are wonderful and clearly illustrate my oft-stated opinion that the RV lifestyle is not one thing, but many things, many views. And you can have it on your terms. It is whatever you want it to be—a matter of choosing how you want to go about using an RV.

Last week, we did Quartzsite, Arizona, again. To reiterate my advice in this column only a year ago, this is a place with an event that most RVers should experience at least once in their lifetimes. In a ranking of large RV gatherings, Quartzsite is in a league of its own. Family Motor Coach Association, which has the next-largest gathering, hosts a huge national rally with around 6,000 rigs; Quartzsite has 50,000! See what I mean?

With a zillion or two acres (Bureau of Land Management–administered land) on which to park, Quartzsite is a great place for family and friends' mini-rallies. This year, ours was one of nine rigs pulled together in a circle. Every night we shared a potluck and a campfire. Evening entertainment consisted mainly of talk about nonserious subjects like RVs (lots of comparisons and "getting-fixed" stories), places we've visited, places we hope to visit, people we've met, and lots of darn good jokes. It's hard to beat campfire talk.

Typical of boondock areas, shopping at Quartzsite is not a prime pastime; rather, it is done only if one has to have a loaf of bread or a quart of milk. Of course, flea-market devotees have a super blast; after all, Quartzsite bills itself as the world's largest flea market. But it's about fifteen miles to real stores.

There are other factors that some might consider negatives about the Quartzsite kind of camping. One of them is bumpy dirt roads (actually trails that wind around the creosote bushes) and parking on bare ground, which presents some difficulty in keeping your RV, clothes, equipment, and yourself clean. The dirt-churning of thousands of vehicles on those roads creates less-than-perfect air quality. Also, rationing water and holding-tank space and meeting power requirements are problems that are alien to full-hookup RVers. It isn't all hearts and flowers out in the boonies.

On the other hand, it's wonderful, but not perfect, here at this fabulous resort. Streets are paved, clean, and fifty feet wide. Hookups are 50-amp (with cable and phone), good shopping and restaurants are nearby, as are several great attractions, including golf courses and all kinds of services that we take for granted in urban areas. However, the traffic is sometimes horrendous (why are city people always in such a hurry?), and airport noise sometimes stifles conversation.

One thing is quite noticeable to me: The residents of this resort—many of whom now live in park models—seem to have lost some of the friendliness that so typifies the average RVer. I am accustomed to exchanging "Hi, ya's" when I walk past another RVer; that doesn't happen as often here as it does out in the boonies when you meet someone.

I guess when you give up your wheels, some things change—not all to the good. When you're regularly mobile and you're the friendly type, you have to communicate with strangers, since you don't see people you know on a regular basis. Apparently when you settle in at one place for a long period of time, you lose the urge to communicate with people you don't know because you have plenty of people in your life that you already know. Possibly, too, being around lots of people you don't know brings a return of the feeling of fear and distrust of strangers that is so typical of city people.

My point is that there's something about the real outdoors, with accommodations provided by Mother Nature, that brings about a spirit of neighborliness that is sometimes missing in the partly-manufactured outdoors. Perhaps the lesson is that we should occasionally renew our acquaintance with the simple pleasures that come with hooking up to the great outdoors. Or, on the other hand, regardless of where we are, what kind of RV accommodations we are partaking of, or how many strangers we are surrounded by, we should remember the spirit of friendliness that has always been characteristic of RVers and greet every-one with a cheerful, "Hi, ya!"

You'll find the spirit catching.

■ ■ ■

August 1997

The Curiosity Factor

L ike cats, RVers are a curious lot. In fact, an essential ingredient for becoming one is to have an insatiable curiosity about people, places, and things. They're the kind of people who want to know about the world they live in—what's over the hill, around the bend, and where a road goes. They keep maps handy to grab whenever they hear the name of a place they aren't familiar with.

By way of contrast, there are the old poops whose thinking processes are in hibernation most of the time; they don't think and they don't do. Their lives lack excitement because they're not curious about the world in which they live. They seldom go anywhere, and their usual response to questions beginning, "Would you like to . . . ?" is, "No."

A clear indication of the wanderlust affliction that RVers suffer from is our preference for homes with wheels. Whether we're fulltimers, extended-timers or free-timers, we insist that our abodes—temporary or permanent—be mobile. Why? Because we want to be able to take our homes with us to places that we're curious about. Our curiosity urges us on, but we want the comfort of our homes as we satisfy that curiosity In short, we want to have our cake and eat it too. And we get that with our motorhomes.

Gregariousness is a normal characteristic of motorhomers. We're friendly people who like people. Why? I guess it's because we're curious about others. We're interested in hearing their stories about who they are, where they've been, and where they're headed. Swapping information is a favorite pastime when RVers get together. A group sitting under an awning on a hot afternoon in Yuma or Mission or Winterhaven, sipping cold beverages, often finds the subject of conversation is about places that the RVers have visited and enjoyed. Sharing that information stirs up the curiosity genes, and the seeds of adventure are planted then and there. So often I've visited a place because another RVer described it in such a way that I just had to see it for myself, and I know I have been responsible for many trips by others. It's the only way to satisfy curiosity

RVers are curious about the world—its history, geography, geology, and other aspects of this planet and the life on it. Often you see RVs in the parking lots of museums, historical places, unique geological sites, and beautiful scenic spots. Proof of this observation is clear if you take a look at the parking lots of those places, many of which have signs designating special RV parking areas.

The curiosity of some RVers is so pronounced that they take advantage of every opportunity to learn more about the RV lifestyle. That fact is definitely proved by the number of RVers and wannabe RVers who attend every class or seminar about the subject of RVing that comes their way. Actually they'll go to great lengths to participate in special events, as witnessed by the demand for space at the annual Life on Wheels Conference at the University of Idaho and the extension programs in other states. Many couples drive clear across the continent to attend these classes. Insatiable curiosity, that's what it is.

Curiosity goes hand-in-hand with the spirit of adventure. It is a catalyst that moves people to action. For example, a couple listens to a story by a fellow RVer about a trip to Mexico; their curiosity, their desire to see for themselves, and the nerve to tackle the unknown soon have them looking at maps and information books in preparation for a trip of their own.

I think fulltimers are excellent examples of how curiosity can dictate a lifestyle. Giving up "normal" or "regular" life to move into a relatively small cabin on wheels in order to ride off into the sunset on a permanent vacation is definitely an act of daring that demands a very strong curiosity level and a strong penchant for adventure.

The effects of the curiosity factor are quite apparent in the general knowledge that most RVers acquire. Unlike the poor fellow who has an hour's boring commute to his job every day on the freeway, the variety of destinations and experiences of most avid RVers provide them with opportunities to learn about people, places, and things—opportunities that most of them jump at with enthusiasm. And that enthusiasm leads to an accumulation of general knowledge that typifies the longtime RVer.

Speaking of trips, on our annual pilgrimage to points south this winter, Margie and I are planning a side trip to the Tuzigoot National Monument. We'll stay at Dead Horse Ranch State Park. Looking ahead, next summer we're planning to go fishing at Bull Shoals and probably will take a float trip down the White River. And while in that area we'll probably stop at the shirt outlet in Yellville.

Curious people will soon have their maps out. Are you one of them?

■ ■ ■

September 1997

The Ant and the Grasshopper (Revised)

With the dog days of summer soon to be behind us, it's time to start planning to join our winged friends on their annual autumn flight to winter roosts. As the approaching chill alerts those feathered migrants of the need to stock up on energy for the long flight, so we RV snowbirds should make some preparations for our winter sojourns in more agreeable climates.

First, the rig itself. A complete checkup is crucial, and all potential trouble spots should be serviced. Motorhomers who do their own mechanical work should get out the maintenance checklist and make every adjustment, change fluids, install new belts, inspect every critical point carefully, and generally make sure the rig is in perfect shape long before their anticipated leaving date. Those who rely on others for maintenance work should schedule an appointment with a qualified service facility to get the work done. The time and money you spend on preventive maintenance can save a great deal more time, money, and aggravation as you travel later.

The same detailed checkup is a pretty good idea for ourselves, that is, a thorough physical examination before leaving home. Although most snowbird roosts have good medical facilities, generally we feel more comfortable with the opinions of our longtime family doctors. A checkup might reveal an actual or potential problem that should be addressed before we take off for several months. It might be that prescriptions need to be filled to last for an extended period of time.

Experienced snowbirds usually don't have a problem with arrangements for accommodations at their winter destination. Since they usually go back to the same places year after year, they've learned that the best procedure is to reserve their space on an annual or seasonal basis. That assures them of a spot where they want to be when they get there. As an added benefit, long-term rates are the least expensive.

Neophyte snowbirds, on the other hand, may not know where they want to settle for the winter and can't make advance preparations like those who know what they want to do. They definitely should decide on a general course, however, and make some reservations well in advance (like now) for at least two months.

The reality is that most of the parks in the major snowbird areas—Arizona, Florida, the Rio Grande Valley of Texas, and Southern California—are already solidly booked for January and February. So, even though you aren't really sure where you want to be during those months, it is a good idea to commit yourself to a place. It is possible that the park you reserve space in might not be quite what you would have chosen if you'd had the experience of being there before. But the alternative might be to find yourself spending a lot of time reading No Vacancy signs as you search for a spot to settle in to enjoy your share of the sunshine—or paying first-rate prices to park in third-rate parks.

Without actually having been there, the next best bet in choosing a specific spot is to (1) select an area that has characteristics that you particularly like, for example, desert country (Arizona) or tropical country (Florida), and try it first; or (2) choose a place where others you know are staying. It's great to have a guide to show you the ropes in a strange place. If you are a desert lover, you really can't go too wrong in making a reservation anywhere in southern Arizona, and if you like a more tropical climate, you'll probably like almost anywhere in Florida. The point is that you can base your choice on some of your general preferences.

Another example: If you like desert country but deplore cities, perhaps you would be better off to reserve at Casa Grande (a small town between Phoenix and Tucson that is fast becoming a major snowbird roost) rather than Mesa, or in Florida, choose a park near Avon Park or Sebring (small towns and open country) over one in Tampa–St. Petersburg. In short, you can set criteria for making an intelligent selection to try out.

On the other hand, you might be the derring-do type that just can't commit to a definite place at a definite time. Like some of my friends, you prefer to stay just wherever you happen to be, whenever you happen to be there. I've had my share of that kind of travel over the years. Sometimes the accommodations are sparse rather than choice, but, as I have often said, "I have never missed a night being somewhere."

I guess the moral to this story is that if you are inclined to be a bit on the conservative side—like the practical ant—you should make a reservation, but if you are more the adventurous grasshopper type, you'll enjoy your carefree jumps, but you should expect some rough landings.

■ ■ ■

October 1997

Campfire Memories

E very once in a while, I think about campfires—not just any campfires, but specific fires that have pleasant memories associated with them. Sitting here at my computer, I can look back over a long lifetime of blazes that still warm my bones.

When I was a country boy growing up with four brothers in southern Illinois, the campfire was a staple feature of our forays into the woods. Sometimes we tested our cooking skills on various kinds of game.

Once, with the aid of one of our country schoolmates, my brothers and I killed a possum. Although we had never tasted possum, we decided to roast our kill. The campfire was built, we cut forks, and then put the skewered victim over the blaze and eagerly awaited a sample of what we envisioned would be a tasty morsel. Unfortunately our notion of what constituted "done" was a bit off, and our first bite of a scorched, rubbery leg of nearly raw meat quickly dispelled any visions of a possum feast. But it was a great campfire.

The Maxwell family, like most motorhomers, started camping the conventional way, with tent, sleeping bags, and campfires. Since we lived in Southern California, year-round outings were possible. As our three kids grew up, they learned that the campfire was very special. I'm sure that when they reminisce about some of those trips, they can visualize the flickering flames at some of the places we visited in the mountains, in the desert, and at the seashore.

I can recall a night at Edison Lake with my son, a couple of nephews and their dad, and Grandpa. It was incredibly dark among the huge pines and more than a bit on the cool side, so the campfire was particularly welcome. With all those rather awestruck, wide-eyed boys, I couldn't resist telling some ghost stories. Since we were surrounded by huge, somewhat spooky trees, I came up with a goody about "the tree that walked," accompanied by gestures and weird sounds. I soon had those wide eyes even wider as the boys edged closer to each other— and Dad and Grandpa. I can still picture those nervous boys around that campfire nearly forty years ago.

Our family had a tradition of camping at Thanksgiving. Usually we went to the Anza-Borrego Desert with several friends who had folding trailers, which had become our big step up from the tent. Since there was no firewood available, we took plenty with us for a fire in the old tub we took along for a firepit. Everyone had kids, so there were probably a dozen or more and an equal number of adults around the fire each night. With a sky full of stars, it was a grand way to spend an evening with friends and kids.

Some of our best campfires were at El Capitan State Beach. We went there every year for a week when our kids were growing up. Learning early that if each of our three kids took a friend they had a better time, we always had six youngsters with us. However, as if those six weren't enough, our generous kids were always bringing newfound friends to our camp for dinner. I can recall one particular night when Margie counted fourteen gathered around for spaghetti. The kids were a bit older then, so their new friends were of a similar age. A couple of the fellows had guitars, and they played and sang around the camp-fire that night. It was indeed choice living.

I used to go fishing a lot with my son. We didn't need much fancy equipment—just our fishing tackle and a minimum amount of gear. I remember once when we went way back into Kennedy Meadows on the east side of the Sierra. We found a beautiful spot along the river and set up our camp: a tarp, sleeping bags, one pot, a can of spaghetti, and a campfire. We built the fire so that we could put our backs to a big rock.

I heated up that spaghetti, and we had a feast, just my boy and me sitting by that campfire and enjoying the solitude. You can't beat that.

One of my favorite pastimes while camping used to be sitting by the campfire and reading after everyone else had turned in for the night. I hooked a Coleman lantern behind my chair to a special pole. Although the fire kept my front side warm at high elevations, a jacket was often necessary. I can still picture one night at a High Sierra campground when I was reading Bruce Catton's *A Stillness at Appomattox*. A campfire at my feet, a good book in hand, puffing on my pipe (a habit I gave up thirty years ago), a tad of brandy in my glass (also given up), and my small son snoozing nearby—it doesn't get any better.

Although I don't get to enjoy as many campfires nowadays, we had some dandies in Quartzsite, Arizona, last February. With our "wagons" in a circle, we were among a dozen friends around a fire, telling some raunchy jokes. Campfire camaraderie has changed, but it's still pretty darn good.

■ ■ ■

November 1997

Forging Friendships

T here's no easier way to meet people and develop friendships than by living the RV lifestyle. If the creation of friendship is a step-by-step process, then over half of these steps are skipped by the motorhomer who pulls into a campground space near a group of other motorhomers whom he has never met before. Even before his rig is parked, the new neighbors are waving and waiting for him to join them. The friendship process has already started.

I don't know whether it's because RVers have a special gene that makes them naturally gregarious or whether the lifestyle conditions them. Either way, RVers don't seem to meet strangers. Greetings and conversations come naturally and quickly. Often those easy contacts lead to a long-term association or deep friendship.

It doesn't take an Einstein to figure out why RVers easily relate to their fellow man. As people with a unique approach to life (we drive our houses, which makes us kindred spirits), we understand a lot about each other before we get down to the details. The reality of our lifestyle is such that we either connect quickly or we don't connect at all. Therefore, it is perfectly understandable why we don't waste time, greeting each other on sight and acting as though we are longtime neighbors in short order.

All normal people have friends and family with whom they are involved as they work and play in their "regular" lives. But as people become more involved with motorhomes, they also become more involved with other RVers. Their common interests, as a result of their lifestyle, lead them naturally to doing things together. And as with most people in most circumstances, the more one motorhomer knows about another and the more they share experiences, the stronger their bonding becomes.

Just as many old friendships wane with the passing of time and the changing of place and circumstance, so friendships tend to blossom with new experiences, in new places and new circumstances. You don't have to give up old friends; you simply add new ones. You still maintain contact with those old friends, but the time spent with them must be shared with your new RV buddies.

Undoubtedly, the most important feature of friendship is conversation. Young people talk about their work (their job experiences, the raise they're expecting, their rotten bosses), their kids (how smart they are, their accomplishments in school, their clothes, their athletic abilities, how mechanical they are), and their toys (furniture, gadgets, vehicles). When they reach middle age, their subjects of conversation are much the same.

When they become motorhome owners—usually in their more mature years (unfortunately, few young people can afford RVs)—the topics of conversation change little among women (their grown kids and the grandkids), but men talk almost exclusively about their motorhomes (comparing features, engines, transmissions, how fast they can go uphill, average mpg, various problems, and how to avoid them). The point is that people usually have the same interests they had in previous stages of their lives.

Even if it's for short periods of time, motorhomers make contacts almost anywhere they happen to be. Long-term friendships frequently begin at RV gatherings (club rallies, conventions, and RV shows) and at special events that attract large numbers of RVers (football games, auto races, dog or cat shows). Without jobs or conventional household chores, RVers can take time off from the event to chew the fat under the awnings of each other's rigs, meet for attitude-adjustment gatherings, sightsee together, and sample the local eating establishments. That mutual interest in fun activities is a wonderful bonding cement.

Undoubtedly the best opportunities for establishing friendships with your fellow motorhomers come while caravanning, especially on long trips over extended periods of time. For example, Margie and I met two couples that we especially liked on a caravan in Mexico twenty years ago. We've visited each other many times since (we were snowbirds together in Yuma for several years) and have maintained communication on a regular basis.

The only thing different from the friendships that we enjoyed when we were young is the range of topics of our conversation. Now we talk about our aches and pains, our most recent operations, our finances, supplemental insurance, Social Security, and acquaintances who have recently died. Of course, we're still bragging about the kids, only now it's our grandkids and great-grandkids.

We motorhomers have a lot in common, including great friendships.

■ ■ ■

December 1997

Freedom

As a twenty-year student of fulltimers, I have learned a book-full of information by asking a lot of questions of those who have opted for life on the road. Chief among them is: What is the main thing you get out of fulltiming? Although answers vary to some extent, they almost always contain the word *freedom*. Which, of course, leads to further questions such as: What do you mean by freedom? Freedom from what?

Generally, answers relate to the restrictions and constraints, real or imagined, that circumscribe "regular" living. Whether or not they realize it, people who live in houses, especially in cities, are limited by the society in which we live. To a certain extent, we have to be on our toes much of the time because of community conventions. In short, we are expected to behave in a certain manner and observe rules of behavior that are somewhat restrictive if we are to be considered normal.

Another type of restriction is imposed by ownership of real estate. Anyone who doesn't understand that possessers of houses are also possessed by those houses has never owned a house and properly cared for it. The chores that go along with home ownership are endless: mowing, trimming, fertilizing, painting, repairing, remodeling, etc. And the bills that go along with those chores are equally endless, plus the added expenses, such as utilities, taxes, and insurance. Indeed, house owners are required to spend much of their time and energy working to earn money to maintain their abodes.

Another factor that restricts many people who own homes is the threat of neighborhood crime. In fact, in many towns and cities, people must worry about burglary and vandalism every time they leave their houses, even for short periods. Proof of that condition is the number of houses that have special locks on the doors and iron bars on the windows.

Many fulltimers comment on the fact that living in a community for long periods of time leads to limited choices for doing new and exciting things. Just think about it, you folks who have lived in the same house for thirty years: Not that having the same people, places, and things in your lives every day is necessarily bad, but it is restrictive. However, for many people, that way of life leads to days lacking in sparkle. Certainly the quality of life is determined a great deal by our surroundings.

Many of the limitations that are encountered in a normal lifestyle are lifted by full-time life in a motorhome. In an economic sense, the financial burdens of house ownership are dramatically changed. I have had more than one former homeowner who is now a fulltimer tell me that the cost of maintaining his home had escalated to the point where his retirement income would not support his house. The reality is that living in a motorhome can be considerably less costly. Being free of the economic burden of house ownership is indeed an important casting off of the ball-and-chain of normal living.

One of the freedoms frequently mentioned is the opportunity to be where you want to be, but still have your own home and your possessions. Specifically, people who formerly lived in places where the climate is inclement for several months a year now have the freedom to move with the sun to warm sites—and become snowbirds. They have the opportunity to move quickly and easily if they don't like their location, whereas the homeowner is stuck where his or her house is.

Fulltiming gives you the opportunity to be with people you enjoy at times of your own choosing. Most of us have friends and relatives scattered throughout the nation, and there's no better way to visit them than in the comfort of your own (motor) home. Fulltimers plan to see kids and grandkids regularly; some even plan to spend entire summers, when the weather is good, making the rounds in their former home areas. In fact, it isn't uncommon to hear that they see their relatives more often now than they did when they lived "regular" lives. What's even better, they visit while living in their motorhomes without inconveniencing anyone.

Another freedom they frequently mention is the freedom from boredom—the means to make life exciting by experiencing new places and new things. Living in a house requires the development of many routines, some of which are quite boring. But, with the freedom to travel by simply turning the ignition key, and with the abundance of exciting places to visit, the fulltimer has many choices about how his life will be spent.

Fulltiming may not be the perfect way to live, but for most fulltimers, this way of life can be summed up in three words: Free at last!

■ ■ ■

January 1998

RV Show Biz

As the song goes, "There's no business like show business." And there's no better show than the big September event in Harrisburg, Pennsylvania. Officials of the Pennsylvania RV and Campground Association (PRVCA) know how to give the RVer what he or she wants and needs. If it isn't actually the biggest and best RV show in the nation, it is certainly up there with the top three. That's a conclusion I've had no trouble arriving at after many years of participating in RV shows all over the nation.

The two-day trade show that precedes the public show gives RV manufacturers an opportunity to introduce their new models for the coming year, and most take it. Consequently, Harrisburg is, in effect, a "coming-out" party for dealers as well as consumers. Although the State Farm Complex is huge, it actually bursts at the seams with RVs for the event. Indeed, it is an opportunity for those who are shopping for a new RV to see more brands and models in two days than they could see in weeks of shopping at individual dealers.

Ideas about what an RV show should be vary a great deal. In many cases, it means showing RVs. RV manufacturers, dealers, suppliers, and campground operators offer their products or services to attendees. Making everything available in one place creates a department store of things connected with the RV lifestyle, which makes shopping easier. Also, it gives prospective buyers an opportunity to learn about new products and services available to them, presumably at bargain prices. All shows are an effort to bring sellers and buyers together in a special good-time, bargain-day atmosphere. But some shows offer another dimension: education about the RV lifestyle. No show host does a better job with that aspect than the PRVCA.

Margie and I have toured the country with our RV-lifestyle program for many years, so we've had an opportunity to see firsthand the approach that different show promoters take. In most instances, our seminars are the only educational segment of the show. In a few cases, however, they are part of a larger program designed by show directors to help and encourage people to enjoy the RV way of life (and, of course, to spend more money on RVs, accessories and supplies).

Nowhere is that attitude more apparent than at Harrisburg, where the executive director and the board of directors of the association understand that education about RVs and RVing is an important ingredient in an RV show. Let's take a look at what was offered one year.

My seminars were only a small part of the total program, along with a tech expert and several other specialists in such topics as insurance, travel with kids and pets, and RV weight considerations. Actually, the seminar program was so extensive that you could spend most hours attending them.

A special added attraction to this show really gave people an opportunity to combine RV shopping and seeing all the new products with learning how to use those RVs and products. It was the Life on Wheels Conference that preceded the RV show. Students at the University of Idaho extension program were offered forty different courses taught by fifteen instructors, all of whom are experts in RVs and RVing. Although the program will be offered in other parts of the country in months to come, the PRVCA was the first to step up to the plate and offer it to their customers. In short, they understand the value of having educated consumers.

Although the school was held at the Harrisburg Area Community College, it just happens to be across the street from the State Farm Complex where the RV show was held. Attendees were permitted to park their RVs in the complex parking lot, where they camped for three days prior to the show. Most stayed there for a few more days for the RV show afterward. The two events flowed together, much to the enjoyment and benefit of everyone concerned. The students had easy access to the show, and the dealers and suppliers had enthusiastic and more knowledgeable consumers to deal with. According to reports from some of the students, they felt more comfortable plunking down deposits on what was, for most of them, the second-largest purchase they had ever made in their lives. Education made the difference.

The fact that attendees of the Harrisburg show are permitted to park their RVs in the parking lot has become so popular that more than half of the available space was occupied by RVs. Fortunately, another large parking lot across the road takes the overflow. However, it is advisable to arrive on Wednesday or Thursday, see the show, and leave before the weekend, which tends to become very congested.

Information about the Harrisburg RV show and the Life on Wheels Conference can be obtained by calling PRVCA at (800) 732-2226.

■ ■ ■

February 1998

Highway Horror

O n a sunny afternoon last September, on two-lane highway U.S. 95 just a few miles north of Winnemucca, Nevada, we stared death in the face. Closing at a rate undoubtedly exceeding 100 miles per hour were my motorhome and a large cargo truck moving directly into our lane.

Unbelieving, I shouted, "Get over! Get over!" but the monstrous vehicle kept coming. A horror that has taken hundreds of thousands of lives, including those of some of my friends, was about to happen: a head-on collision between two huge machines and the almost certain death of Margie, me, and the truck driver.

But it didn't happen. Fortunately I apparently judged our closing rate well and kept my speed up, knowing that if I slowed down the truck would be over far enough to hit me for sure. Aware of a gravel shoulder that sloped down, I feared that veering off would topple our motorhome. I knew, though, that I could take to the sagebrush field at the last fraction of a second if I had to. In vain, I kept hoping that the driver of the truck would realize the situation and pull back into the right lane. At a fraction of a second before we would collide, I whipped off the road. We missed by inches, and I made it back on the road without a scratch.

I had no time to look at the driver of the truck, but Margie did. She said it was a woman driver who was slumped over toward her door. As I watched in the mirror, she pulled back into her lane and proceeded on her way. Apparently she had been asleep, and my honking air horns as we passed awakened her. She didn't stop, and neither did I. Probably she was as dumb-stricken as we were for the next few miles. Surely she realized that we had, only by the narrowest of margins, averted a terrible tragedy.

Actually, the full mental impact of this near tragedy didn't hit me until that night and for several nights thereafter. In nearly sixty years of driving, it was the closest brush I ever had with a catastrophic accident. As a long-time defensive driver, I almost subconsciously try to antici- pate moves that I could make to avoid a collision with a vehicle that has suddenly moved into my lane. Driving down the highway, I play a game of watching approaching vehicles and asking myself what I would do if one started coming at me. When my game-playing became a reality, I can still clearly recall my thoughts when I first saw the truck edging into my lane. I knew I had options, but I waited until the last possible moment before I exercised one. It worked that time, but I hope I never again have that challenge. Believe me, game-playing with other driv- ers has taken on a more meaningful aspect.

This close call has caused me to take a fresh look at my life. Again game-playing, I pose to myself some questions: "What if the worst had happened? What if Margie and I had been killed? Who and what would have been affected? Have we made the worldly preparations that are within our control?" My conclusion was simply that I would leave a lot of messes for someone to have to cope with. Which leads to the obvious question: "What do I need to do now?"

For example, our wills are approximately twenty years old and a lot has changed in that time (some of it good, some not so good). Those changes and additions that Margie and I have talked about from time to time (the "we-oughtas") should be taken care of right now. By mak- ing those revisions before something happens, some of the problems that our executor would otherwise have to cope with will be avoided.

Another subject that should be addressed is any projects I am work- ing on, to assure their completion or continuation, particularly those that involve other people. Any ongoing negotiations involving sales or buying should be known to someone who could make decisions that would bring the situations to satisfactory conclusions. In short, provisions should be made for answers to all the questions survivors or executors would have to face.

It has been two months now since the near-tragic episode, but I still think about it often. Every big truck that I meet on the highway brings back memories. I suspect that I will see that white cargo truck in my mind for a long time. Although it does not make me fearful of driving, it does make me more conscious of the fact that our near-disaster is an actual disaster every day in many places. That knowledge will keep me more alert every time I hit the road. My experience, perhaps, will encourage you to do the same.

And I hope the lady truck driver who dozed off and nearly ended all our lives also has the experience indelibly etched in her mind and has become more attentive to her driving.

■ ■ ■

April 1998

No-Hassle,
No-Haggle Pricing

I hate shopping for a new car. I love looking at the wonderful new machines, but it rankles me no end to have a salesman hovering over me and prodding me to say those magic words, "I'll take it." He's just doing his job, which is to get the sale at the highest possible price, and I, the buyer, must spar with him to get the lowest price. As with the gladiators of ancient times, it is not an encounter in which you want to be the good guy. Good guys often lose, and this is one of those cases. It's a fight to the finish over dollars, a contest in which an unskilled buyer gives more of his dollars than he has to for the merchandise involved. Why should a buyer of any commodity have to enter into a mental wrestling match when all he wants to do is just buy the product and leave with the feeling that he has not been taken?

But, "the times, they are a-changin" in the car business. Saturn manufacturers started it with their new product and a new way of selling. Each car has a sticker, and on that sticker is not only the manufacturer's recommended retail price, but the actual selling price. Instead of concentrating on how to get the most money from the customer, the salesperson focuses on the product. Instead of questioning the customer about what it would take to make a deal, he or she provides information about the vehicles and tries to show that they are good values. It's selling the product, not the price.

I've solved my problem by (1) not buying as many cars as I might if the chore weren't so onerous, and (2) buying only from a friend in the car business who shows me the invoice and tells me what he has to have. However, there's a trend in the automobile business which suggests that, in the future, more dealers will be "value-pricing," that is, following the Saturn act with one price—no haggle, no hassle. In short, they're going to bring straightforward honesty to automobile selling.

To a limited extent, the RV industry is also pointed in that direction. In the past few years, several RV dealers have experimented with a "one-price" program (again, referred to as value-pricing). Some have succeeded; some haven't. The dealer's goal is to show enough profit to stay in business.

All RV buyers are looking for the best deal, which means that they usually shop at several dealerships for the lowest price. They will pit one dealer's price against another's, trying to get each to bid lower than the others.

In that scenario, the dealer who has a firm price up front could be at a disadvantage, because any competitor can price his product a few dollars lower and always be sure of getting the sale. The challenge for the value-pricing dealer is to convince prospective buyers that buying from him is better for the customer in the long run; for example, better service, more fringe benefits, closer location, etc. Many buyers value such factors more highly than they do a few more dollars in initial cost.

In my judgment, they are smart. Having super service after the purchase is, in the long run, an important part of motorhome ownership, which suggests that where you buy should get strong consideration, along with the way you buy and how much you pay. Ideally, a motorhome buyer wants to find a dealership that has a single price, but also the lowest price, the best after-sale service, and a location near his home. Dream on!

One of the dealers' problems in value-pricing is that consumers want a firm, low price on what they are buying, but they want unrealistically high prices on their trade-ins. Well, it's a two-way street. Those trade-ins have to come in at realistic prices—what dealers call ACV (actual cash value), or what they would pay for the unit if they were buying it outright to resell. However, some buyers consider what the dealer offers for a trade-in of paramount importance. An offer of $30,000 for your old rig, which has a resale value of $20,000, as a trade-in on a new one priced at $80,000 may sound great. You've made an extra $10,000, right? Not if a value-pricing dealer has that same new unit priced at $60,000 and offers you a trade-in price of $15,000 for yours. On the first deal, you pay a difference of $50,000; in the second, the difference is $45,000. Which is the better buy? Think about the difference, not how much you'll be given for your trade-in rig.

Fair, honest, no-haggle, no-hassle value-pricing is, in my opinion, the best way to buy and sell products. Whether or not it will become the norm for the RV business remains to be seen. For consumers who like to haggle, there are plenty of opportunities, and I'm sure there always will be. But for those of us who like to know exactly where we stand when making big purchases, give us more value pricing.

■ ■ ■

May 1998

What's Your Purpose?

What is your purpose in life? That's a question that everyone, even retired Rvers, needs to think about occasionally. Going through life without purposefulness is more like existing than living. Everyone needs to feel that the fact that they are on this earth is of some importance, that it matters whether they are here or not. There should always be something that we are working toward; not necessarily any particular kind of goal, but something that gives meaning to our life. We should have the feeling that there is a reason to get up in the morning other than the fact that it is 7 o'clock.

Having purpose in life doesn't mean having an uncontrollable urge to save humanity or any other noble objective, but it does suggest that, in order for your life to be meaningful, you need to be aware of the world around you and have a desire to make some imprint on it.

Just about the finest compliment is when someone says, "You made a difference in my life," or, "The world is a better place because of you." Even little things, perhaps, can be indelible in their effect on the lives of others. All of us can think of people who influenced us, who made our lives better. Just try making a list of people you remember as being important in your life—and why. Very simply, those people left an imprint on you. Then you might try making a list of people on whom you believe, or at least hope, you have made some imprint.

I suppose that most of us at times consciously think about what we are doing, where we are going, and what we would like to accomplish. Whether it's serving as a camp host in a public park where you get free space along with your modest duties, or leading a crusade to improve education in the public schools, is beside the point. Although the objectives vary enormously in significance, both give you some responsibility for doing something that makes life a little better for others, which in turn gives your life purpose. It gives you an opportunity to make a positive difference.

However, having purpose doesn't necessarily mean that you have to be doing something for others; you could be doing something for yourself. For example, you might have a hobby that you pursue regularly. You enjoy making or doing whatever it is, and you strive to improve at it. Perhaps it is something that you can share with others, like making furniture or painting pictures, but that part is irrelevant. The main thing is that it brings joy to you; it is something you look forward to doing. It gives you purpose.

After a lifetime of having a job, raising kids, and coping with the multitude of challenges that go along with living for sixty-five years, retiring to the rocking chair is a sure way to begin the end. All kinds of studies show that people who become inactive, physically and/or mentally, take a shortcut to the grave. Apparently the human body needs to have reasons to keep functioning. The body muscles need to be exercised and the brain must be challenged. We regularly hear and read about individuals of very advanced ages who are performing incredible physical and mental feats, such as athletic teams comprised of eighty- and ninety-year-olds and people of similar ages writing books or teaching.

Recently I saw a TV news segment featuring a company that hired primarily people over sixty-five years of age, indeed some in their eighties, to work in a needle factory. The boss had praise for their competency and reliability as workers. And interviews with some of the workers indicated that they were very happy with their jobs. They had purpose in their lives.

Conversely, I'm sure we all know people who don't appear to have any real reasons for getting up in the morning. They have no jobs, no hobbies, no sports, no activities either mental or physical; they don't read; they don't participate in clubs, associations, or causes. They sit a lot, staring off into space, or they amble about aimlessly. Their conversation consists of only the most perfunctory comments or mumbles. Usual responses to invitations to participate in some activity are, "No," or, "Not today." Some of them watch television, or at least have it on, a lot; others doze frequently In short, their lives are without purpose—empty. Often those lives end prematurely, possibly from sheer boredom. Some aren't very much missed, simply because they didn't make much of an imprint on the world around them.

So, how do you make sure you don't end up in the "blob" category? Simply by being a participant in your world, having goals, being a doer. Look at your life and ask yourself what you like to do, what you want to do, and what you can contribute to those you care about.

Then do it!

■ ■ ■

June 1998

Looking Back

T
ime slides by so unobtrusively One day were in our thirties, playing with our toddlers, and the next we're applying for Medicare. A question that folks of my generation often ask is, When and where did it all go?

It's amazing how one decade blends into the next. Marvelous changes occur; we quickly accept them and incorporate them into our lives as everyday things. So it has been with the RV industry for the past three decades—the time that basically covers the youth-to-maturity period for motorhomes.

I've had the privilege of being a part of the RV industry for nearly forty years. I got a dealer's license in 1959 so I could sell camping trailers at my camping-equipment store. When I saw those machines, I just knew they would click with the camping public.

Unfortunately, my customers did not get excited about those trailers. I think I sold one the first season. However, it was the beginning of something that eventually caught on with the public as folding trailers became more sophisticated. Heck, by the mid-sixties, they even had stoves, iceboxes, and two beds off the ground! I sold them by the score, which somewhat justified my first impression that many camping families would jump at the opportunity to take some of the roughness out of roughing it.

Camping trailers might have been a step up from the tent, but there were assorted sizes of travel trailers and truck campers for those who wanted more of the comforts of home. Indeed both of those types of RVs boomed in the late sixties and early seventies—especially as they became available with refrigerators, furnaces, air conditioning, and complete bathrooms. The fifth-wheel trailer appeared in the early seventies and was immediately accepted by the public. Oh, what great times for the RV industry! Everybody wanted an RV, and prices and credit terms were such that almost anyone could afford one. In fact, 1972 was the banner year for the number of units sold, and it has never been surpassed.

Motorhomes entered the RV scene in the early sixties. The idea wasn't new, but until that time they were custom-made, expensive, and few in number. I recall being at an RV show with my Nimrod tent trailers (price about $600) in 1965 where a Clark Cortez motorhome was being shown. In my ignorance, I thought it was an outlandish machine for camping and that the retail price of almost $10,000 was right up there with the moon.

"It will never sell," I said. "No one will spend that kind of money for a camping rig. And who wants to be cooped up like that when you are camping?" I was a lousy prognosticator.

One reason they caught on so quickly was that most motorhomes in those days were relatively simple and inexpensive. I remember that the first Pace Arrow I sold in 1970 went for $7,500. It was essentially a travel-trailer type of box mounted on a Dodge truck chassis, not many bells and whistles, just 20 feet of basic shelter that could be driven. In fact, most motorhomes of those days ranged from 18 to 24 feet. But each year they grew a little larger—and fancier. When the big, grand Executive was introduced (I believe in 1970 or 1971), I thought it was a palace on wheels. I don't recall the price, but I think it might have been in the mid-teens.

Other elegant machines appeared at about that time. Revcon, with its revolutionary front-wheel drive, was one. Among others that made a lasting mark were GMC, Apollo, Sportscoach, and FMC. But, like so many brands, they're gone now, primarily due to the great energy crunch of 1973–1974.

Although I was busy as a dealer, in the summer of 1972 I was given an opportunity to apply another interest: writing. I had written many

camping stories for a local newspaper and a few for an RV trade publication prior to this time, but I got an opportunity to write for a new
publication being developed by TL Enterprises. Called *Recreational Vehicle Retailer*, it was directed at RV dealers and other segments of the
industry. That brought me into contact with the people who were
responsible for this magazine, then called *Motorhome Life*, which was
only four years old at the time. That was twenty-six years ago.

Although I sold the dealership twenty years ago, I have been very
much involved in both the RV industry and the lifestyle ever since. I
saw those boxes-on-wheels of the sixties evolve into the magnificent
motorhomes of today. I have been happy and proud to add my two
cents to that process as Margie and I have enjoyed more than twenty-
five years of motorhoming ourselves. And during that quarter century,
I've ground out a lot of words for *MotorHome*, including sixteeen years
for this column.

Happy Birthday, *MotorHome*. I wonder what the next three decades
will bring?

■ ■ ■

July 1998

The Baby-Boomer Effect

The stereotypical fulltimer is a gray-haired retiree living on Social Security, savings, and a pension, who wanders around the country, staying where he chooses as long as he wishes.

Proudly he displays bumper stickers or wears hats claiming that he has no address, no job, no boss, and no responsibilities. His main topics of conversations are, in order of importance: his motorhome (particularly improvements that he has made), where he has been, and where he is going, and his and his wife's most recent health problems.

But "the times, they are a-changin'," and so are the demographics for full-time RVers. In fact, many of the wannabes who attend my seminars and the Life on Wheels courses definitely don't fit the stereotype. In short, they aren't gray-haired, they aren't retired, and many don't have secure incomes. They are younger; some of them are in their thirties and forties! Although still a minor influence, these young people represent a whole subculture of the full-time fraternity.

I can't help but think that some of the attitudes that characterized the young people of the 1960s are still being held today, particularly those that encouraged independence. People who believe that if there is something you want to do, you should "go for it" probably are particularly prone to give fulltiming a try.

Some have been the victims of downsizing in large corporations and have turned their situation of being unemployed into an opportunity to take a new approach to life. Rather than try to return to their previous lifestyle, they have opted to sell out and hit the road full time, using income from the sale of their houses and other assets to fund their new mode of living. Others have suffered burnout from the pressures that come with corporate responsibilities. The full-time RV lifestyle is an appealing way out. I find that I regularly meet this kind of full-timer in campgrounds.

Although some of the younger fulltimers have solved their financial problems, many haven't, so their questions often reflect a major concern about making a living. Unlike the retiree with a guaranteed income, these young people must create paydays as they travel. Those with kids are concerned about the education of their children, and their health care concerns are directed more toward pediatrics than geriatrics.

Another and much larger new influence among fulltimers is the ever-growing group of early retirees, mostly people in their fifties and early sixties, who have performed the required number of years of service for retirement with guaranteed incomes. Others who have managed their finances so that they have become financially independent choose to realize their travel dreams well before the customary retirement age. Although they may not have to supplement their incomes by working, many early retirees simply don't feel that their productive years are over, and they want to do something useful. Some want to continue with work similar to what they formerly did; others prefer to try something new. Still others avail themselves of the many opportunities for volunteer work.

Although most of these early retirees are in their fifties, I recently received a letter from a couple of "youngsters" who are fulltiming at age thirty-one. They obviously had managed their finances well and have given up the security of a business and a home to see the world. However, they are looking for ways to create income to supplement their nest egg. Both have skills that could readily create paydays as they travel.

Most early fulltimers don't have substantial nest eggs and, therefore, have to plan for immediate income. Consequently, the question they ask me first is, "Do you think there are enough opportunities for us to make a living as we travel?" My answer is emphatically affirmative.

Opportunities are plentiful; it is simply up to them to select from the many options they have, and go for it.

For those fulltimers who prefer employment that requires little special skill (just an ability to relate to other people and a will to work will suffice), opportunities abound right in the best RV areas at the very best times of the year. Of course, I'm referring to jobs related to RVing. All popular snowbird destinations require thousands of additional workers during the season. HELP WANTED signs proliferate as the snowbirds gather.

It's too early to gauge the effect of younger fulltimers or others in this lifestyle, but as baby boomers in increasing numbers ride off into the sunset full time, their impact is bound to be felt. I suspect that, to some extent, the older people will simply have to move over a bit and give them room. In fact, I'm sure that many of the younger group's refreshing ideas will put some additional spark in the full-time RV lifestyle.

■ ■ ■

September 1998

What Is an RVer?

R emember the story about the blind men and the elephant? A group of blind men were asked to describe an elephant. One grasped the animal's leg and concluded that an elephant is "like a tree." Another took hold of its tail and logically reported that an elephant is "like a rope." The third blind man felt the point of a tusk and assumed that an elephant is "like a spear." That, in a nutshell, demonstrates the difficulty in perceiving almost anything accurately due to subjective viewpoints based on different points of contact. Perhaps that helps to explain why there are various—some unflattering—perceptions of RV owners.

Perceptions of RVers come from two categories of people: those who are not part of the vagabond fraternity and those who are. The former base their opinions on their occasional contact with recreational vehicles under various conditions. For example, many people never actually get to know RVers as people; their contact is simply that of meeting recreational vehicles on highways or seeing them parked in various types of RV facilities. Following motorhomes that are creeping up steep mountain grades leads some motorists to perceive the occupants of those vehicles as old people who clutter up the highways. Based on their experiences, their observations are understandable.

I had occasion a few years ago to attend a public meeting at which many members of a community expressed negative views of RVers in general. A developer of extremely high-quality RV parks planned to build a new resort in Calistoga, California. A public furor ensued, and citizens of that community were given an opportunity to express their feelings at a public hearing. Apparently none of the residents at the meeting had much acquaintance with RV owners, but they definitely had opinions. Speaker after speaker emphatically described RV owners as people who don't bathe regularly but hog a community's water supply when they occasionally stop overnight at an RV park; who clutter up downtown areas with noisy, smelly machines that pollute the atmosphere and create traffic problems; who spend very little money in the towns they visit; and who are, by and large, an undesirable group. What exactly those opinions were based on I don't know, but it was obvious that they stemmed from limited and often negative contact with RV owners.

It isn't unusual for people who have observed RVers in some shabby situations, for example, old run-down trailer courts occupied by decrepit trailers and broken cars, with toys and beer cans strewn about, to conclude that that is how all RVers live. A phrase that became popular in the thirties and forties to describe migratory people living in trailers was "trailer trash." Unfortunately, that impression stuck with a lot of people, who view today's RVers from that same jaundiced viewpoint. It isn't uncommon for city planning commissions or city councils to dredge up that viewpoint to deny RV-park developers the necessary building permits.

Cities that are deluged with snowbirds usually include some segment of citizenry who perceive their winter visitors negatively. Consequently, during the winter months, when snowbird towns are filled, traffic often moves at a pace slower than normal. Stores may be crowded and checkout lines long. Some local residents resent the inconvenience of having their pace slowed down and blame it all on the snowbirds.

On the other hand, most observers of RVers probably envy them for being retired and able to tour America. Motorhomers, especially, are viewed as rich folks with the time and energy to go wherever and do whatever they please. Certainly a part of the American dream is to join such people as quickly as possible.

RVers themselves differ in their perceptions of their brethren. For example, sometimes people with older, smaller, less-expensive rigs look upon those with newer, larger, more-expensive rigs as elitists who are not a part of the "regular" RV community. Conversely, the "trailer trash" view still has popularity among some RVers who see what they perceive to be substandard ways of RV living.

The reality is that RVers are as different as people who live conventional lives. They vary as widely in their rigs and lifestyles as people who live in any normal community. Some are rich; some are poor. Some have million-dollar motorhomes; some have trailers worth a few hundred dollars. Some poke along on the highways; some are speed demons. Some are very considerate of their fellowmen; some aren't. To lump them all into one neat category simply won't work.

Maybe my eyesight is less than perfect, but from my standpoint as a nearly four-decade participant in the RV lifestyle, I've concluded that most of us are pretty dang nice.

■ ■ ■

November 1998

Getting Even

O ne of the great opportunities that comes with full-time or extended RVing is that it gives parents a chance to get even with their children. Anyone who can remember those teeth-gritting times during their kids' teen years, particularly, might want to avail themselves of this chance for payback. As an old expert about these things, I'll share with you some tips on how it works (tongue in cheek, of course).

First, make a surprise visit to their house. Don't tell them when you are arriving; just pull in the driveway and honk the horn. When your daughter or son runs out, yell, "Surprise! We're here and we're hungry!" Hook up to their electricity and water and turn on a half-dozen lights, even if it's midday, plus the television and a radio. If your transmission leaks a bit of oil, don't bother to put cardboard or paper under it. When you go into their house, be sure to (a) leave the door open, or (b) slam it shut.

Arriving inside the house, go directly to the refrigerator. Open the door wide and just stand there, silently staring at the contents. If it is your son's home, finally grab the milk and drink directly from the carton. If someone asks you what you are looking for, say, "Oh, nothing. I was just looking."

When snack time comes (which should be several times a day), take things like crackers or cookies with your drink into the living room. Drop lots of crumbs on the floor, and be sure to put your glass or soft-drink can directly on the coffee table, so it will make rings. If you fix something like a peanut butter and jelly sandwich, definitely do not put anything away. Leave everything on the counter, including plenty of dabs of the ingredients you are using and the dirty silverware. When you finish eating in the living room, leave your glass or can and plate on the coffee table or on the floor beside your chair.

A definite get-even point can be scored by plopping yourself into your son's favorite chair, where you settle in for the evening. Grab the remote control and tune in C-Span or an infomercial on carpet sweepers. Turn the volume up and relax, while totally ignoring muttered pleas for a more exciting channel and lower volume.

Few opportunities for revenge against a daughter who was a picky-picky eater at home equal that of being a dinner guest in her house. Although various approaches may be taken, one of the basics is to take some of everything, but don't eat some things. Just push them around your plate with a fork—back and forth, back and forth. Be sure to have a sort of sour-pickle look on your face. If she asks why you aren't eating, tell her, "Oh, I'm just not hungry." At your son's house, be sure to leave quite a bit of food on your plate. If you accidentally clean up your plate and are full, ask for a couple of things anyway. Then just take a bite or two, and leave the rest.

At your son's home, be sure to work on something in his garage. Get out all his tools, saw some boards, paint something—anything that will make a mess. When you are through, just leave everything where it falls or where you were finished with it. Definitely leave the sawdust, paint rags, and other messes for him to clean up.

By all means, at your daughter's house, gather up all your laundry— towels, clothes, bed linens, and especially any grimy coveralls used while fixing things under the motorhome —and plop it on the floor in front of the washing machine. Just leave it there.

One of the really great methods for getting even as you travel is not to write or call for weeks at a time. Let them worry about where you are, and smile smugly as you remember all the times when you worried about where they were and how they were doing. And when you finally do communicate with them, be rather vague about your plans for the immediate future. Maybe you'll go to Maine, or maybe it will be Mexico.

Definitely, but definitely, get a bumper sticker that reads, WE'RE SPENDING OUR KIDS' INHERITANCE. Rave enthusiastically about all the wonderful places you've visited and those that you expect to see in the future. Don't miss opportunities to comment on how much all this costs and how you worry sometimes about running out of money. That will really shake them up.

Stay long enough at their houses so that they develop bags under their eyes, have nervous tics, and look utterly exhausted. Just for kicks, make occasional comments about staying for another month. But when you feel that they're at the breaking point, announce that you are leaving for parts unknown. Just watch that look of relief come into their eyes as you kiss them good-bye.

Incidentally if anyone knows the whereabouts of my three kids, would you mind telling me? They moved and forgot to leave forwarding addresses.

■ ■ ■

December 1998

Christmas on the Road

Some families, especially those with small children, think that snow and fireplaces characterize the Christmas scene, but many extended-time RVers just don't accept that stereotype. Although it is not unusual for some snowbirds to rush home for the holidays, many don't. And most of those who choose to stay wherever they are don't suffer when they hear the plaintive lyrics and notes of "White Christmas" that fill the airwaves on December 25.

As RVers who have spent many of the past twenty years without the traditional Christmas fixtures, we can assure you that we don't miss out on the joys generally associated with that special holiday time.

Although we are the parents of three offspring and the grandparents of six, we have found that life does not end if we don't have them with us on December 25. In fact, we have had some wonderful times with RVing friends who find themselves in the same boat—er, motorhome—when Christmas Day rolls around. Surrounded by our contemporaries, with interests that match ours, seated under an awning on a warm sunshiny day while savoring a bit of Christmas cheer—life just doesn't get much better.

One of our best-remembered Christmases was in 1991, when we were parked at River Ranch, a luxury RV resort in central Florida. Since we had visited the park several times before, we had friends there—many of whom, like us, did not choose to join the hordes of folks who feel compelled to spend Christmas with their families. As one who believes that the term *terminal illness* was invented by a linguist who was forced to travel regularly by air, only the most imperative situations force me to take that mode of travel. We are perfectly content to join our friends wherever we are and "make festive," which is what we did seven years ago.

A Yuletide tradition that had sprung up at River Ranch was a parade of decorated golf carts on Christmas Eve. Many resident RVers have carts at River Ranch, as do those at other RV resorts with golf courses, so the parade was quite long. And as might be expected, there was much competition for the best-decorated cart. Wending their way around the streets in the resort, preceded by a fire truck with a ringing bell, the gaily decorated carts, many with music playing, beckoned everyone to enjoy the parade. From the front seats of our motorhome, we took in the cheerful scene and felt very Christmasy indeed.

The next day we went with two other couples to a beautiful golf-resort restaurant for a magnificent Christmas Day buffet dinner. I have never seen such an incredible display of food—every kind of traditional meat, vegetable, fruit, dessert, and beverage—done up in the most appetite-whetting way. To say that we did justice to the chef's superb efforts would be a huge understatement.

Since even large motorhomes with relatively huge storage spaces can't hold everything, we don't take along much in the way of Christmas decorations. Many years ago, Margie bought a foot-high stuffed Santa Claus, which she puts on the dash, and that is our sole adornment. Margie does the shopping for presents for our kids and grandkids as we travel. Since we are frequently in towns where unique crafts, clothing, and knickknacks are sold, she usually finds special goodies for everyone. Those gifts are mailed weeks before December 25, so there is no last-minute rush.

Actually, we don't always find ourselves without family at Christmas. Like many families, ours has members scattered all over the United States. Depending on where we have been on holidays, we've enjoyed the company of our children and grandchildren, brothers and sisters, nieces and nephews, or, for many of our RVing years, our parents.

A most memorable Christmas was the one several years ago when Margie and I drove our dinghy up from Florida to Illinois through a terrible cold spell (it was −13°F in Nashville as we drove through) to have Christmas dinner with our mothers. As it turned out, it was the last time for that special occasion. It probably would not have taken place had we not been RVers.

Another special Christmas was in 1985 when we were staying in a newly opened park in Yuma, Arizona. Most of the occupants were snowbirds who had settled in for the winter. To enliven our first Christmas together, all of us decided to have a gift exchange, with Santa Claus doing the honors. A retired professional football player, who did not require additional padding, played the part of St. Nick. Of course, a potluck preceded the gift exchange and a dance followed. I don't think any of us suffered greatly from being away from our families.

Yes, Virginia, Christmas is for families—but aren't all RVers family?

■ ■ ■

January 1999
Don't Be an Ugly RVer

General perceptions of large groups of people are sometimes shaped by only a few of those being judged. However, those few sometimes exhibit behavior that is so inappropriate it is recorded indelibly in the minds of those who feel wronged by their actions. So it is with motorhomers whose unthinking, unknowing, or uncaring driving habits have earned for all of us the unflattering sobriquet "ugly RVers."

On the other hand, fortunately, there are motorhomers whose careful, courteous driving habits create an opposite view. From the standpoint of common courtesy and safety, it behooves all of us who ply the highways with our rolling homes to be at our best when we are behind the wheel. By doing so, not only will we create positive images of our lifestyle, but we will improve our chances of traveling without damage to our machines and our persons.

Perhaps a review of some of the most common motorhome driving dos and don'ts will be useful to those who care about how their neighbors on the highways feel about them, as well as their own safety.

- *Stay a safe distance behind the vehicle in front of you.* That distance will vary according to your speed. When you are going 65 miles per hour, that distance needs to be 200 feet or more. Obviously, you won't be able to keep that distance in crowded road conditions, for example, when you are climbing hills at slow speeds and in cities where cars will keep cutting in front of you. However, it is crucial that you give yourself plenty of stopping distance in case of an emergency. As all experienced motorhome drivers know, our big vehicles do not stop quickly.

- *When passing another vehicle, do not cut back in too quickly.* Carefully calculate your distance from the vehicle you have passed and move over slowly after signaling well before you start.
- *When overtaken by a truck, blink your lights when it is safe for it to return to your lane.* Most truckers are courteous; we should return the favor. In cases where they exhibit discourteous behavior, do not lower yourself to their level by doing the same. (Incidentally, I started writing this column more than 2,000 miles ago and have been doing "research" all the way. I have to conclude that most truckers are courteous in all respects.)
- *Pull over when driving conditions require you to drive more slowly than automobile traffic.* When on mountain roads or other roads that require slow driving, watch the traffic behind you carefully and try to avoid holding up anyone. More than any other act of driving discourtesy, the refusal to pull over to let faster drivers pass creates the "ugly RVer" image. Some states have laws that require pulling over whenever five cars pile up behind you; however, it is courteous to pull over if possible when even one car is held up.
- *Stay in the right-hand (slow) lane unless conditions require otherwise.* On many highways in several states, that is the law as well as just plain common sense. One exception to this rule is when you are driving in cities that lack added exit lanes, where driving in the right-hand lane with traffic on the left side can force you onto off-ramps that you don't want. In places where this is the case, it is a good idea to stay in lane number two.
- *Signal turns and lane changes well in advance.* Due to the fact that motorhomes move relatively slowly, it is a good idea to warn other drivers of your turns sooner than you would in a car.

- *Don't park where you impede other traffic.* Most parking lots that we pull into for shopping are large enough for us to park out of the way. We should never try to save a few steps by taking several parking spaces up front.
- *Stay out of the middle of town when possible.* Motorhomes don't belong in busy downtowns, and many locals will let you know it. Not only do we impede regular traffic, but the danger of dings and scrapes to our coaches is much greater than it is on less-jammed streets.
- *Don't hold up traffic behind you by passing other vehicles that are moving almost as fast as you are, especially when going slowly uphill.* Truckers doing that aggravate drivers of automobiles; motorhome drivers doing the same thing infuriate them.

Finally, we should always try to be exemplary drivers for reasons of both courtesy and safety. Fortunately or unfortunately, the very nature of our "beasts" makes us conspicuous on the highways. For better or for worse, we are always on display, inviting judgments by other drivers. It is up to us to put our best road manners forward, so that positive conclusions are made about us and our driving. That way, we can dispel the "ugly RVer" image among those with whom we must share the highways.

■ ■ ■

February 1999

Old Dogs and New Tricks

An old saying claims that you can't teach an old dog new tricks —an adage that is frequently applied to human beings, particularly those who are more mature. Unfortunately, there's a lot of truth in that saying, as is obvious from the apparent reluctance of so many of us to change the habits that we have spent so many years developing. We're comfortable with the old way of doing things; we feel secure in eating the same foods, wearing the same kind of clothes, using the same products, getting our hair cut the same way way, and going to the same places where we do the same things we have done countless other times. Many RVers fit that mold.

There's something to be said for sticking with a winner. If you've taken your motorhome to a great RV park in a great place where there are great people to associate with, it's an understandable temptation to go back again and again. Many motorhomers, for example, use their rigs as summer cottages that they move to the same parks in the same spaces nearly every weekend every summer.

In the case of retirees, many go to the same snowbird park every October, taking up where they left off the previous April. They've found a comfortable niche, so they stick with it. All factors—people, activities, expenses, weather, etc.—are known. Altogether, it's not a bad way to do things. The only things left out are new places, new people, and new experiences, and that can have a stifling effect on your life.

I suppose there are some people who would not benefit from any changes, but most of us occasionally need to deviate from the beaten path. If we believe that variety is the spice of life, we have to change habits and patterns now and then so we can sample some of the infinite variety of choices RVers have. We don't have to give up our friends and stop going to places we like; we should simply add some new ones now and then.

Most motorhomers, even those who are still punching a time clock, have many good choices open to them when it comes to choosing RV destinations. To prove my point, just take a map, pinpoint your location, and draw a circle with a 100-mile radius from that point. Look at the map carefully and note the number of specially designated parks, historical sites, or other points of interest within that circle. Public campgrounds are indicated on most maps, and by using a *Trailer Life Directory*, private campgrounds and RV parks can be located, many with descriptions of local attractions. A goal might be to visit each of those places and at least know what is available in your own backyard.

Some snowbirds lock themselves in to one roost and never deviate from the same rigid schedule every year. Not that it is a bad thing to keep returning to the same places and parks that you enjoy, but it does restrict the spirit of adventure that gets most motorhomers into the lifestyle in the first place.

Just to make sure that we aren't missing out on some great experiences, perhaps we should all review our game plan occasionally to make sure we aren't overlooking something. Maybe we should point our noses in new directions now and then, and test the waters in other roosts. Since there are so many places where snowbirds gather, it follows that each of those places must have something special to attract all those "birds." Who knows—it could be that one of them might even be better than the place you've settled in. But you'll never know unless you do some experimenting.

If you have special friends that you want to be with regularly, a good way to have your cake and eat it too is to caravan together to new places. You can have new adventures, but still enjoy your buddies. Of course, traveling together requires compatible people. Deciding how fast you'll go, what roads you'll take, when you'll stop, where you'll stop, and for how long means that you'll not always travel exactly the way you would have preferred. But the neat thing about it is that even as you drive along, you can chitchat via the CB and enjoy each other's company. Stopping at night means pleasant get-togethers: happy hours, potlucks, sharing thoughts about what you've seen and done, and, of course, planning for the next day. That sharing of ideas can often lead to a great experience that would have been missed had you chosen to travel on your own.

Perhaps a useful exercise for all of us would be to take stock of where we've been and where we haven't gone yet that we would like to go. Particular attention should be paid to the latter. Maybe it would be a good idea to make a list of all the "want-to-do's" and tape it in a conspicuous place in our motorhomes, just to remind us that there are new experiences waiting for us to find. That means that if we've been locked into a pattern, we need to find the key to get out—and show ourselves that we aren't too old to learn new tricks.

■ ■ ■

April 1999

The Old Folks at Home

A difficult situation faced by most motorhomers at one time or another, particularly those who are fulltimers, is trying to balance their chosen lifestyle with caring for aging parents. Since the average age of most extended-time motorhome owners is Social Security, it is a fact that those with living parents have old parents. Often that means parents who have health problems that limit their activities to the point that special attention is required. Frequently that means assisted-care living or nursing homes. But even if the parents remain in their homes and care for themselves, the fact of their advanced ages influences their children to want to be with them as much as possible. How to balance that urge along with the lure of the open road presents a dilemma.

In interviews and discussions with hundreds of motorhomers throughout the country over the past three decades, I have heard innumerable stories about coping with aging parents. In fact, just today I received news that a good friend's mother has passed away. My friends are avid motorhomers who had restricted their travels considerably in the past few years to care for the mother—an option presented to thousands of RVers at any given time. For various reasons, the responses differ. Some folks put their RVing plans on hold and devote their attention to their parents' care; others put their parents in nursing homes and take to the road. Rationalization for the former is that "my parents come first," whereas the latter conclude that "there's nothing I can do to make matters any better, so I might as well do my thing while I can." Obviously, as with all interpersonal relationships, those between parents and their offspring vary greatly. Some are very close and need to have each other's company often, while some don't have close emotional ties and seldom see each other.

I don't know what the statistics are, but it seems to me that most motorhomers have lived much of their lives in states different from where their parents live. Consequently, there has long been a separation in miles between parents and children that has created a significant time-and-expense factor in getting together. As long as the parents maintain a house, the children can always "go home" and have a place to stay. However, when the parents move to an assisted-care facility, there's no longer a home to go home to. When visiting their folks, the motorhomers, who can almost always find a camping spot close to the nursing home, definitely have the edge over those who must bear the expense and inconvenience of staying in hotels.

Although there are no easy or perfect answers to questions of how to meet the challenges of coping with aging parents, Margie and I worked out our answer long ago. When her parents were in their seventies and in relatively good health and fond of travel, we took them on some motorhome trips. My long-widowed mother took one long trip with us when she was in her late seventies. However, most visits occurred at their homes, where we had plenty of room to park our coach. Fortunately my mother and Margie's parents lived within ten miles of each other, so we could visit all of them at the same time. As they grew older, our visits grew more frequent. When her parents opted for a nearby retirement home, we were still able to see them daily while staying at my mother's place.

After Margie's father passed away, we made it a point to see her mother even more regularly. One of our favorite times was Thanksgiving, when we used to pick her up and take her to my mother's house where Margie would fix a big dinner for the two old ladies who had known each other for so many years. It was a very special time for us.

Those days are gone now. My mother passed away four years ago, and Margie's mother is in a nursing home. She's ninety-nine and totally incapacitated by a severe stroke. We've been staying nearby for almost two months. Margie goes in every day and spends several hours with her—washing her face, rubbing her with creams, combing her hair, stroking her face, feeding her lunch, and talking to her, even though she doesn't always respond. But the point is that Margie is with her mother, doing what she can to make her comfortable at a time when there can't be many days left. That is very important to Margie and to me.

We have undoubtedly missed seeing some wonderful places and meeting some nice people because we chose to spend a great deal of time with our parents in their declining years. But we gained a lot more. We were able to share in their daily lives as those lives became more restricted. I'm sure they enjoyed their time with us; we know we enjoyed our time with them. I'm glad we had the opportunity to be with them— and took it.

New places can wait; old folks can't.

■ ■ ■

May 1999

Expectations
Versus Reality

Couples who are newcomers to the RV lifestyle sometimes bring
with them expectations that are as unrealistic as those held by
most newlyweds. Neither can visualize the bumps that most will
encounter as they navigate the actual highways of America or the figu-
rative highways of life. Fortunately, most participants will cope successfully with whatever problems and challenges they encounter and take
delight in the people, places, and things they meet. Unfortunately, some
don't have the flexibility to bend when realities don't fit their expectations, and the result is unhappiness and failure. Whether it's RVing or
marriage, the real winners are those who can "go with the flow."

As forty-year veterans of camping and RVing, I think Margie and I
have had most experiences—good and bad—that can be encountered
on the road or in the woods. I'm not sure that we had any specific expectations in the beginning; things just sort of developed as trips took place.
Although we always had some special things we wanted to see or do, we
learned early in the RV game that there was no point in trying to
make everything about each trip picture-perfect. In short, we learned
that to be happy as RVers, we had to be prepared to endure some "warts"
along with all the good things that the lifestyle affords.

I raise this subject not to be negative about a lifestyle that has brought
us countless pleasures over the decades, but to encourage novices to
face some facts that confront all RVers. An awareness of some potential
problems can provide opportunities for the mental, if not the physical,
preparation for coping with them. On the other hand, the unaware ide-

alist with expectations that don't fit the real world may find some of his RVing experiences dream-shattering.

Probably some overly optimistic expectations are created by writers and teachers, like me, who almost invariably write and talk about the good side of RVing. You can't blame us, though, because, after all, who wants to hear a story about a trip to a terrible place or having an awful time? No one. So our stories are about wonderful places and great times. And we include pictures of marvelous scenes that are guaranteed to make you want to go there and see for yourself. It's those good stories and the great RV experiences described by relatives, friends, and neighbors that help create RV-lifestyle wannabes. Throw in the glitzy ads of incredible motorhomes parked in idyllic places, and it's no wonder that beginners come in with expectations that do not include mechanical breakdowns, crummy campgrounds, noisy neighbors, poor fishing, or bad weather. Having some idea of the problems that you might face allows for preparation for coping with those problems.

For example, probably the greatest source of pleasure for motorhomers is also the greatest source of grief: the motorhome itself. Unfortunately, those beautiful, wonderful, complicated, expensive machines are prone to breaking down—especially if they are not maintained or operated properly. Because of the potential for problems, the realist prepares as best he can to avoid them. First, he knows his machine—how to treat it, how to care for it, and how to fix it when necessary. He reads the pamphlets that come with the motorhome and follows the factory's' recommendations for service. He reads technical articles, attends seminars, and talks to experts. In short, he learns all he can about how things work, how to care for them, and how to use them most effectively. Not everyone can learn to overhaul an engine, but everyone can learn to use a dipstick.

Campgrounds that don't meet expectations are a big cause of distress for some RVers. Campgrounds come in a variety of conditions, shapes, sizes, features, and prices, just as hotels do. Some are incredibly elegant, with amenities that match those offered by expensive country clubs, whereas others are havens for the stereotypical "trailer trash." Most are somewhere in between. By referring to the current *Trailer Life Directory*, you can get a pretty good idea of what to expect. Basically, it's a case of getting what you pay for. Our solution to the less-than-acceptable campground that we occasionally find ourselves in for the night is simply to pull the drapes. Regardless of the circumstances outside, our motorhome always looks the same inside.

A third source of disappointment for some RVers are the sights they came to see. Regrettably, not every scene in nature matches that of Yellowstone Falls from Artist's Point. However, that doesn't mean that these sights aren't worth seeing. The secret, we've found, is to enjoy the little as well as the big, to look at whatever good there is in most things, and to accept the imperfect when there isn't any way to change it.

■ ■ ■

June 1999

Is Mexico Dangerous?

Recent reports of robberies and assaults against foreign tourists in Mexico have tremendously impacted RV travel south of the border. Some estimates indicate a drop in tourism of at least 30 percent—a significant reduction in income for those businesses that depend on foreign currency, especially U.S. dollars.

My recent two-week visit to mañana land substantiated those estimates. When I see empty spaces in parks during the peak season, I don't need an accountant's report to tell me that all is not well. Whether or not the drop is due to crime reports isn't clear, but discussions that I hear around RV gatherings definitely indicate a big concern about personal safety in Mexico.

Are the reports of crimes against American RV travelers true? Some of them, yes. Apparently there have been a few very isolated cases of bandits holding up motorhomers and trailerists. On the other hand, thousands of RVers are traveling unmolested. The fact is that the few cases of banditry that did occur made the news and created an impression that simply isn't true. Like the recent robbery-murders of foreign tourists in Florida, the few incidents that actually occurred made headlines in other countries, and some people there jumped to conclusions without looking at the total picture. To say that it has now become unsafe for foreigners to travel in the United States is ridiculous; it is equally absurd to believe that RV travel in Mexico has suddenly become dangerous.

Much of the problem is due to the human penchant for exaggeration and rumor-spreading. Plans for coming to our country were cancelled because people were afraid of being robbed and murdered. Overlooked is the fact that hundreds of thousands of foreigners have traveled here without being criminally assaulted. Statistics probably show that foreigners are safer here than those of us who live here. Whether or not that is true about Americans traveling in Mexico I don't know, but I do know that the thousands of Americans we saw in Mexico last week appeared to be very unconcerned about their safety. Quite the opposite; all appeared to be quite relaxed and seemed to be enjoying themselves immensely.

I won't pretend to be an authority on travel in Mexico; it would take much more time and mileage than our recent trip. However, I had the good fortune to be traveling with some experts, and I think I can make some general recommendations based partly on what I saw and partly on what I learned from others.

First, do not buy the idea that Mexico is a country one should steer clear of because it isn't safe. However, be realistic when you travel there. In our country, there are places where you don't go and things that you don't do. Every big city has areas where no stranger is safe, so few of us go there. To do so is to invite robbery—or worse. It's the same in Mexico. In the cities, you don't wander off the beaten path unless you know what you are doing. In the country, stick to the paved roads and follow a map.

Second, travel with someone seasoned, especially if you are a first-timer or have apprehensions about being there. It's the old story: Two heads are better than one. In fact, I recommend that you travel with a professional caravan. Not only do you have the advantage of a guide who knows the country and its people, but you have someone to do the planning so you can see the most and best with the least amount of work on your part. However, those who are experienced travelers in Mexico will tell you that it's no big deal to do things your own way if you prefer that route. Tens of thousands of Americans go south of the border every winter by themselves without fear and without problems.

Third, take the right attitude with you. Many Mexican people are much poorer than most of us, but they aren't inferior. The barrier of language keeps most of us from really enjoying these friendly, happy, intelligent, and delightful people, who will respond in kind to positive overtures. We had the good fortune to be traveling with a family who had spent a great deal of time in Mexico, spoke Spanish passably well, and knew many restaurant and shop owners. It was a pleasure to observe how delighted they and their Mexican acquaintances were to see each other again.

Finally, be a giver part of the time, not always a taker. We took small gifts, such as pencils, notebooks, balloons, toys, and games for children we met in villages and at an orphanage. Mexican children are so beautiful, and it was such a pleasure to see their joy at receiving our gifts.

My point is, if you have been thinking about traveling in Mexico, don't put off going because of the horror stories. Remember this: The crime rate in Mexico is a heck of a lot lower than it is in the good old U.S. of A.

■ ■ ■

July 1999

Next Time

Like so many other people, I have a good share of procrastination genes that keeps me from doing some of the things I'd like to do—or should do. For example, in our travels, we frequently are made aware of special places or things that we would really like to see, but for one reason or another we pass by, and I say, "The next time we come through here, I'm going to stop." I'll bet there are 5,000 places that I've said that about. In fact, some of them I've gone by several times over many years and made the "next-time" vow repeatedly.

Then there are wonderful places where we've spent a day or two and moved on when I really didn't want to leave. We had to because of what seemed to be something more pressing. So many times I've remarked, "The next time we stop here, I'm going to stay longer." Unfortunately, many of those places are on roads that I never have—and probably never will—go down again.

And speaking of roads, often I take the same road to a particular place when there are alternates that might be more interesting. I look at maps when I'm thinking about a trip that I've made before, pick a new route, and say, "The next time, I'm going to go this way." Usually I don't really do it, though. There's comfort in staying on a good road that you know, especially with a big motorhome.

I renege a lot on promises too, unintentionally, of course. Whether it's something I promised Margie I would do (or not do), or something I promised one of the grandkids or other family members, I have a tendency to forget so quickly. Usually I try to cover up those broken promises with promises about something bigger or better next time.

Heck, I even break promises to myself. In fact, I've used that "next-time" excuse a zillion times in the last few months as I think about the next meal. Those extra pounds that I've put on in the past few years need to go, and I keep thinking about losing them. The problem is that immediate opportunities to enjoy good food (not good-for-me, just good-tasting) are presented that I can't resist, but I do make promises about the future. Why, I'll even have to procrastinate one more meal after today because I've been invited out to a fancy restaurant for dinner tonight. I wouldn't think of offending my host by not eating heartily. But I do mean to start cutting back tomorrow.

I've had occasion to regret my oversight or procrastination when it comes to maintaining my motorhome, too. Not lubricating properly, not maintaining the correct fluid levels, and not servicing or replacing things that are worn have caused me untold grief over the years. Every time I have a problem—particularly if it is something that could have been avoided—I vow that next time, I'm going to take better care of my rig and equipment. I must be getting better because I haven't had any trouble for six weeks now.

Of course, this "next-time" business isn't something that just started happening in recent years. When our three kids were growing up and did things they shouldn't have, we straightened them out with dire warnings of what would happen to them the next time they transgressed. It worked, too, and now we have three great kids who use the same method on our grandkids. Ooohhh, that threat about what awful punishments will happen the next time they get out of line works like a charm every time.

We've had a lot of motorhomes over the years, and we tried each time to get the perfect one. We never did, though; otherwise, there wouldn't have been so many "next times" about changes or additions for the next rig. Unfortunately when I declare those "next-time" differences, I don't write them down and hence have forgotten them by the time the new rig is ordered. But that's all in the past. The next time, I'm going to compile a list as we go along and, by golly, I'll present that list with my order. That means that the next time I get a new rig, you won't hear me saying anything that even vaguely suggests that I overlooked the most minute detail.

When it comes to what we pack in our motorhome each year, we deserve the booby prize for the goofs we make. Our program for the past twenty years has been to spend about equal time in our motorhome and in our home in northern Idaho. That means we have to pack every late summer for a six-month-plus stint on the road. Never a winter goes by without scads of vows about what things we're going to include and exclude the next time we pack. I would be willing to bet that I've declared for at least nineteen years that the next time I won't bring so many shirts, but somehow I always end up with about three or four dozen in my closet (by actual count today: thirty-eight).

Now, I've gotta rush this column on its way via e-mail, since the deadline was yesterday. But next month . . .

■ ■ ■

August 1999

Never Say "Never"

One of the questions I always address in seminars on fulltiming is, What do I do about my dog? My answer is, Take it with you, but be willing to do two very important things.

First, you must agree to give the dog the attention that it deserves. For example, be willing to stop according to its schedule, take it for walks, and romp with it. In other words, have your touring schedule geared to the dog's needs.

Second, give your fellow campers the consideration they deserve. It is particularly important that you not only obey campground rules—using a leash, walking in designated pet areas, picking up after your dog, and not allowing it to bark—but also carefully consider the attitudes of people you come in contact with. The fact is, some dog lovers don't understand that not all other people are dog lovers. Some have allergies that make proximity to dogs irritating. Others simply don't like dogs, and they resent it when unthinking or uncaring dog owners allow their animals to intrude in their lives.

Although I don't think Margie and I would have any problem with the second requirement, it is the first one that always kept me ending my pet commentaries with the statement: We will never travel with a dog because we don't want it to control our lives.

Guess what? I'm eating crow. We now have a dog.

Suzie, an eleven-pound mixed-breed, came into our lives unexpectedly. While visiting my sister and brother-in-law in San Dimas, California, last March (we park our motorhome in their driveway), a scroungy-looking little dog showed up one morning. Her fur was dirty and matted, and she looked hungry and scared. Obviously, she was lost.

Although we were sorry for her, we shooed her off. But the next day, she showed up again. On the third morning, we determined that we had to do something.

Our first action was to take her to a dog groomer for a haircut and shampoo. When I picked her up later, I was amazed at the transformation. Not only was she a cute little thing, but a very affectionate personality emerged, and she began to get under my skin. The next stop was at a veterinarian's, where she got a checkup and medical attention for an infection. After a stop at the pet shop for food, a collar, and a leash, it was back to the motorhome and time to make a decision about her future.

Incredibly, that little dog's attitude changed completely. No longer the scared, sad-looking thing we first saw, she happily bounced around and fitted herself in as if she belonged there with us. However, I refused to give her a name because I felt that implied ownership.

Since it was apparent that the dog was accustomed to affection and attention, we tried every avenue to find her owner, but we didn't succeed. A call to the animal shelter produced only an offer to take her in. Knowing how most animals end up there, we couldn't do that. Our next effort was to find someone who wanted her. It took four days, and by then we were more than a little bit attached to that happy puppy (two years old, according to the vet). It was with regret that we turned her over to a nice lady who already had a dog, but wanted another one.

Two days later, she called us and asked to return the puppy, explaining that two dogs were more than she could cope with. We were not too upset to see that little mutt bounce right back into our motorhome just like she had come home. I looked at Margie and declared emphatically, "That's my dog." And that is how Suzie came into our lives.

The next week at my sister's gave us a chance to get broken-in. Instead of getting up in the morning and leisurely sipping my first cup of coffee while watching the news, I now get an early-morning walk even before the coffee is made. Suzie likes to start her day with action, which means I start my day with action too. One of my bad driving habits got corrected on our first trip with her. I like morning driving, so it's normal for me to get behind the wheel and drive for four hours without a stop. I now pause every couple of hours at rest stops—even in the rain. Not only does Suzie get her exercise, I get some too. That's a win-win situation.

We sometimes have to fly and hotel it for several nights at a time. And occasionally we have to be at functions that go on all day, even over several days. I don't know how we're going to cope with Suzie's needs at those times, but somehow we'll do it.

I've learned a big lesson. Some things are just meant to be. So I'll never say "never" again.

■ ■ ■

Being Thankful

Thanksgiving is almost upon us again, so it's a good time to do a little serious thinking about the first part of that big word. Most of us have a lot to be thankful for, but, like a lot of other folks, I sometimes either look at the negative side of things or just plain forget how good my life is. So, to get very personal in a very public way, I'm going to look at my life in terms of what I should be thankful for.

First and foremost, I'm thankful for Margie, my bride of over a half-century. To say that she has been a good wife would be a major under-statement; she has been—and is—a great wife, a super traveling buddy, as good a friend as one could ask for, and my sweetheart. I sometimes shake my head and marvel at the fact that that cute little freshman in high school (I was a sophomore) and I have lived together for over fifty years, raised three kids who have given us six grandkids, shared the good times and some bad times, and she still puts up with me today. As the kids would say, "She's awesome!" And I love her dearly.

I'm thankful for having three great kids and those six grandkids. It's great to have friends all over the country, but nothing can equal having your own family. They're all special; we love them and look forward to our visits with them. We also know we can count on them when we need them.

I'm thankful that I live in the USA. No other country in the world offers what we have here. In terms of nature's bounty, this land is a bonanza. Seacoasts, mountains, deserts, plains—we have it all in abundance. We are blessed with agricultural land aplenty, vast lodes of minerals in the ground and climates of one's choosing, and great economic and great recreational opportunities. Very simply, our geographical heritage has made ours a land of abundance. Nature has been kinder to the United States than anywhere else in the world.

And there are more man-made wonders. When it comes to theme parks, amusement parks, entertainment creations, and engineering and architectural marvels, we are the world leaders. We have more and bigger monuments to man's creativity than any other country, and I have enjoyed seeing so many wonderful things. Best of all, I'm not through yet, for which I am most thankful.

To enable people to see all the wonders our country has, we have a highway system that allows us to travel almost anywhere quickly and safely. I'm grateful that in our country, you can reach almost any place in a motorhome. I am also grateful that we live in a democratic country and have the freedom go and come as we choose.

I am thankful for the opportunities I have had during my lifetime to take care of our family's financial needs (with Margie's help, of course). Not only have we been able to care for the basics—food, clothing, and shelter—but we have had the wherewithal to own motorhomes, to travel, and to enjoy the RV lifestyle for nearly four decades.

I'm thankful for reasonably good health (at least, as my doctor says, good for my age). Thanks to modern medical accomplishments, things that could be quite serious aren't. With the help of a few pills every day, I'm up to most ordinary physical challenges. Also I'm grateful for the abundance of good medical facilities around the country, so no matter where I am, I can pretty well count on help being available when I need it. On a few occasions, we've had to use emergency-care clinics, which we found to be easy to get into and which offered good treatment when we got there. Heck, six years ago, I even had to stop in Sacramento, California, for five heart bypasses. Also, I'm grateful for our national insurance program for seniors (Medicare), which takes care of the major financial burden of medical attention.

Of course, I'm enormously thankful for the fact that we live in the only country in the world that accommodates our kind of recreational vehicle and the lifestyle that goes with it. Motorhoming is a major aspect of my life. I've had motorhomes for so many years (twenty-seven) that I don't know what I'd do without one. So much of our lives has been spent in motorhomes that they are simply a part of the way we live. In fact, very shortly we take off again for nine months on the road. We'll visit friends and make some new ones; we'll visit relatives and help Margie's mother celebrate her 100th birthday; and we'll see some more of this great country of ours. No doubt I'll even pick up some new ideas for columns to share with you.

Finally, regular readers of this column who are dog lovers will appreciate the fact that I am very, very thankful for Suzie, the little lost Heinz 57 dog that adopted us a few months ago. She's our first RV dog and she has certainly changed some of our ways of RVing. And we love every minute of it.

Thanksgiving is indeed a good time for motorhomers to look at the big picture and realize how much we have to be thankful for.

■ ■ ■

Our Lifeboat

I don't know what I have done to anger her, but Mother Nature appears to be exacting revenge for some real or imagined malfeasance. In the past ten days, I have been flooded out of my space at one place and blown out at another. Right now, as I sit in my motorhome in a Wal-Mart parking lot in Charlottesville, Virginia, drying out, I can't help but wonder what my offense was and what to expect next.

During the Harrisburg, Pennsylvania, RV show where I was giving seminars, I was parked in the exhibitors' parking area. It is low land and has a pond just behind it, into which excessive water pours during hard rains. Unfortunately, that pond fills quickly and overflows into the parking area. That was happening when someone pounded on my door during the night and told me to get out fast because flooding was imminent. He wasn't kidding. Quickly donning a pair of pants, barefooted and shirtless in a torrential downpour, I have never gotten a motorhome under way so fast. It's a good thing I did, because the next morning two vehicles that had not been moved revealed how damaging floodwaters can be. Water up to its windshield totally ruined a truck. A fifth-wheel trailer was flooded up to the bedroom overhang. It, too, was totaled. I suffered no damage, but it was very apparent that Mother Nature was after me. I eluded her that time, but another threat was yet to come.

Following the Harrisburg event, we were scheduled to visit my sister, who lives near the coast in North Carolina. We knew that Hurricane Floyd was lurking out in the Atlantic off the coast of Florida. Although Margie was very much against what appeared to her to be a direct challenge to Mother Nature, I stubbornly refused to change our original plan. That proved to be a mistake. With relentless fury, the hurricane spun its way up the coast toward us. After one night at my sister's, we fled again, bowing to forces beyond our control. And that's why I am, at this moment, parked with a dozen other refugees from the storm in a Wal-Mart parking lot.

Actually, we would prefer a campground, but campgrounds in this part of Virginia are all located under big, beautiful trees. With high winds predicted, we definitely do not want to be where those trees or their branches can be blown down on our motorhome.

Although we are very regular customers of Wal-Mart, this is the first time we have had occasion to avail ourselves of their policy of allowing RVers to use their parking lots in some locations for overnight stops. Verification of the validity of that policy is borne out by the fact that we have already spent more than $100 in the store, and Margie and my sister are still in there! I talked to some of the other RVers parked nearby, and they also have availed themselves of the convenience of shopping just a few steps away. I suspect that stopping regularly at Camp Wal-Mart might prove very expensive in the long run, so I don't think I'll make it a habit.

Actually, these recent experiences with an apparently vindictive Mother Nature aren't the first attempts on our lives by natural catastrophes. In California a few years ago, we endured one of the frequent earthquakes. Although there was considerable damage to buildings not far from where we were, we came through unscathed.

The fact that we were in a motorhome in all three of these violent episodes made us much safer than people who live in houses. Fortunately, accurate weather forecasting has made it possible for us to know about storms and floods well in advance, so all we have to do is start the engine and move to safer ground. People who live in houses can flee, but they have to leave most of their possessions. And even if their homes are spared from the wind and water, people often suffer in the aftermath of storms from power outages and a shortage of simple necessities, such as water. We motorhomers, however, have all those necessities with us and can generally survive for many days without suffering. In fact, we had prepared for the storm from which we had to flee by arriving at my sister's with a full water tank, empty holding tanks, a well-stocked refrigerator and pantry, a full propane tank, and a full diesel fuel tank. We were prepared for the worst, and it paid off.

If there is a moral to this story, it has to be this: If you live in—or are planning to visit—an area that is subject to natural disasters, you should have your motorhome prepared for survival. As we found out when we experienced the earthquake, a motorhome on rubber tires and air bags doesn't present the danger that a house does. And having only to fire up the engine and head for the hills is an awfully convenient way to cope with a hurricane, fire, or flood.

In a way, our motorhome is our lifeboat.

■ ■ ■

March 2000

Leaving Worries Behind

One of the good things about being an older RVer is that I don't worry much anymore. Like most people, I spent a lot of time in years past worrying about things that were of special concern at various stages of my life..I'm sure many of those worries that plagued me were generic, things nearly everyone fusses about.

For me, most of those worries are in the past. For better or for worse, all challenges were met and are history now. By and large, I'm reasonably satisfied with the outcomes, and those things I didn't succeed with, well, they just don't seem that important now.

As a country kid growing up very poor during the Depression, I suppose I worried some, but I can't recall anything that bothered me excessively. It wasn't until high school that I became, if not worried, at least concerned about some personal things. I wasn't very big or strong and I envied classmates who were. Actually, the Charles Atlas ads were responsible for my worry about my size and strength. I felt that I was the skinny fellow who got sand kicked into his eyes.

But my biggest concern was the opposite sex. I spent a lot of time thinking about girls and worrying how to go about making points with them, particularly a really cute cheerleader named Margie. My efforts paid off, though, and Margie and I celebrated the half-century mark last year.

After a stint in the U.S. Navy during World War II—during which I worried mainly about surviving the war and getting out of the Navy—I had the problem of what to do about a vocation. That worry took three years to resolve and ended up with my enrolling in college to become a teacher. Of course, I worried about writing papers and taking exams during the college years. But everything got done and I finally became employed as a teacher, with a regular paycheck.

Unfortunately, that salary was insufficient to make ends meet; consequently there was always the worry over how to create more income. Margie, a registered nurse, usually solved that one by working nights. We had to cope with the problem of caring for three kids during those early years and, as those kids grew up, the constant challenges they presented, especially in their teen years in the sixties. Talk about worry—we had it in spades. But we, and they, survived.

I learned about economic worries when I left teaching to become a full-time businessman. Starting a business that you don't really know anything about (in fact, not knowing anything about any business) is an absolute guarantee of big-time worries. Most of all, I worried about money, both how to take more in and how to pay what I owed. I never really solved the whole problem; I just learned how to sell more and owe more.

Living in Southern California got to be a worry after thirty years. Smog, traffic, crime, and particularly the fast pace got to be too much, especially after seeing so many other beautiful places as we took vacation trips in our motorhomes. In fact, in the very early seventies, the Idaho panhandle struck us as a worryfree place to live. We began to focus on changing our place and pace.

We solved those two big problems simply by selling the business and moving to Idaho more than twenty years ago. And very much as I anticipated, the worries were left behind—most of them. Even though your kids grow up, leave home, and theoretically take care of their own problems, somehow parents always stay involved. Then they give you another generation to worry about: grandkids. But the pluses far outweigh the minuses, so those worries are minor.

Our chosen lifestyle has a lot to do with our low-worry outlook. It would be an exaggeration for me to say that motorhoming is a cure-all for the problems that come with daily life, but the fact that it offers so many choices about where, how, and what one will do goes a long way toward reducing them. We spend our summers at our home in vacation-paradise country and the rest of the year where we choose to be and with whom we choose to be. We don't worry about unhealthy air (we don't stay in places where that is a problem); we don't worry about traffic (we stay out of cities as much as possible); we don't worry about crime (the RV lifestyle doesn't attract criminals); and the pace is whatever we choose to make it.

Motorhoming doesn't solve every problem, but it does put into action the "out-of-sight, out-of-mind" syndrome. It's hard to be worried when you are standing at Artist's Point in Yellowstone, driving through Monument Valley, seeing Niagara Falls, listening to Andy Williams at Branson, or doing any of the things that motorhomers do.

Yep, as I watch the beautiful sunset here in Florida's panhandle, I'm not too worried about anything.

■ ■ ■

April 2000

Down in the Valley

W hen the leaves turn brown and the wind turns chilly, snowbirds, both the feathered and wheeled kind, go south—
directly south. A favorite roost for snowbirds from the
Midwest is the Rio Grande Valley of Texas. This narrow band of land
that stretches approximately 100 miles from the Gulf of Mexico at South
Padre Island to Mission is a winter haven for an estimated 100,000
refugees from the winter storms that plague the states between the Mississippi River and the Rocky Mountains. "Winter Texans" they're called,
by themselves as well as by the permanent residents of towns with names
familiar to most longtime RVers. Brownsville, Harlingen, McAllen,
Donna, Pharr, San Benito, and other valley towns burst at the seams with
motorhoming refugees for a few months a year. The local merchants are
especially happy about the estimated $350 million that those Winter Tex-
ans spend during their sojourn along the famed river that separates
the United States and Mexico.

We revisited the valley after a hiatus of about a decade and found
it to be unchanged in some respects, but bigger and better than ever.
Since the area still boasts plenty of RV spaces, relatively modest prices,
and balmy weather, it's not surprising that Winter Texans keep coming
back, year after year.

Actually, we started enjoying our tour before we got to the valley
proper. Having passed through the Corpus Christi area without stopping in the past, we decided this time to take a look at Port Aransas.
What a great decision that turned out to be. Rolling off the ferry that
shuttles between the mainland and Mustang Island, we entered a world
atypical of the Texas stereotype. Port Aransas is a fishing village with

boats everywhere and a wonderful pier where catches appeared to be good. One fellow landed a whopper while we watched, and other hopefuls—many of whom were Social Security age—were reeling in smaller fish. Out-of-state license plates suggested snowbirds at work.

Dining at Trout Street was savored visually and gastronomically. Sitting by windows overlooking the boats at the pier, we feasted on shrimp, oysters, scallops, and fish. The weather was great, the scene before us was awesome, and the food was superb. To make the visit almost perfect, we stayed at a brand-new, better-than-average RV park. The Pioneer RV Resort fronts the Gulf of Mexico, with the beach only a few hundred feet away. As an old Navy veteran, I couldn't resist the opportunity to visit the famed U.S.S. *Lexington*, now a floating museum permanently berthed in Corpus Christi, a half-hour drive away.

Leaving the Gulf Coast, we made our first inland stop at Harlingen, where we stayed in one of the small family-owned-and-operated parks near downtown. We toured many parks in the area; as is the case with most in the valley, 90 percent welcome all types of RVs, as well as park models and mobile homes.

We traveled a few miles south of Harlingen to drive through the area's largest park, the Fun N Sun RV Resort (more than 1,500 spaces) in San Benito. Park prices vary with their quality and amenities, but overall the valley still maintains its reputation as an inexpensive roost. Incidentally, Margie liked the fact that Harlingen boasts a rather large shopping mall.

Wending our way west, we stopped in Mercedes at an upscale resort, Llano Grande Lake Park, where the amenities included everything from Ping-Pong to a golf course. As with many of the valley's larger parks, dancing (square and ballroom) is a popular activity. Again we took time to tour RV facilities in nearby towns. We were most impressed by the Victoria Palms Resort in Donna, which offers first-class ambiance, including a ballroom that could be described as elegant. Also, the adjoining restaurant was much above the average for resorts. Of course, it is definitely not among the lower-priced.

Those who prefer big-city services should consider parks in the vicinity of McAllen, the largest community west of Harlingen. Actually the adjoining town of Mission has the greatest number of RV spaces in the valley, but it is only a short drive to the mall and Wal-Mart in McAllen.

Although the valley's weather is generally near the top of the temperature scale on most days of the winter months, Winter Texans accept the fact that the Gulf of Mexico is nearby, so warm air from the south mixes with the cold air from the north and creates breezes that are sometimes uncomfortably strong. But all snowbird roosts have a downside.

For a complete listing of RV and mobile-home parks in the Rio Grande Valley, call the Chamber of Commerce in Weslaco, (888) 968-2102, and ask for a copy of *The Park Book*.

■ ■ ■

May 2000

Where Do
We Go from Here?

I t happens to every motorhomer. Inevitably you have to hang up
the keys. Then two big questions: What next? And where? Last winter, I had an eye-opener on that subject. Some months before, I had
been asked to speak at the annual convention of the American Association of Retirement Communities (AARC) in Panama City, Florida.
My first reaction was, "No, thanks, that's not my bailiwick." But after
some discussion with the association's director, I agreed to participate
in the program.

What made me change my mind was simply facing the reality that
our motorhoming days are numbered (hopefully not too few), and an
alternative to our decades-old lifestyle will be needed. Although we have
a home in northern Idaho that we visit a few months a year, in all prob-
ability, Margie and I, like most motorhoming seniors, will opt for a new
location under different living conditions for our final home. For many
people, that means moving to a great retirement community—one they
probably discovered during their motorhome travels. And that's what
gave me an idea for a speech that would help RVers now as well as later
when they are thinking about hanging up their motorhome keys.

The purpose of AARC members is primarily to lure retirees to their
communities. If you wonder why, just think about what retirees bring
with them: mainly money! First, they need a place to live—a house,
an apartment, a mobile home, or a condo—to rent or purchase. After
that, it's a lot of give and very little take. Retirees buy groceries, clothes,
cars, entertainment, and services of all kinds. But they don't bring

kids to the schools, they don't commit crimes, and they don't require welfare services. Many bring skills that they donate by volunteering at hospitals, schools, and churches.

In short, retirees generally are a tremendous economic and social benefit to a community. It's no wonder that professionals are busy in many states and cities, working full time to bring those human assets to their communities.

To help those professionals get a foot in the door with RVers, I suggested that they consider ways to make today's RV visitors welcome. I stressed the fact that unless a community makes a favorable impression on first-time visitors, there is little chance that they will return, especially to live there.

One of the best ways to do that, I advised, is to have good RV parks. I urged them to make sure that city fathers who decide issues relating to RV parks and parking understand that RV owners are not "trailer trash." I stressed the fact that cities with strict anti-RV parking laws will most assuredly turn off RV visitors.

I also informed them that not only is the RV industry enjoying good times, but all forecasts are that the boom will continue. I wanted them to understand that the RV industry has a solid foundation and is an important segment of our national economy.

To emphasize the human aspect of the RV scene, I pointed out that there are nearly 10 million RV owners enjoying the life on wheels, and probably a million of them call their recreational vehicles home. And those numbers are increasing. Recent University of Michigan Survey Research Center studies show that baby boomers are interested in RVing and are entering the lifestyle in impressive numbers. Forecasts are for more than a million additional RV owners by the end of the next decade.

Fulltiming is a goal for many, a lifestyle that current RVers are entering at younger ages than the previous generation. Although the average age for all RV owners is forty-eight, most motorhomers are in the fifty-five to sixty-five age bracket—just right to have thoughts about retiring and relocating. Not only are they the right age to cultivate as prospects, but they also are in the right economic bracket. Research shows that the average RVer has an income of $48,000 per year, but motorhomers generally fit into the $50,000 to $75,000 bracket. In short, not only are RVers the right age for settling in new places, but they also have the income to become economic assets to a community.

My closing comments to the group focused on recommendations about how to create good impressions of their communities for today's RV travelers. Among my specific suggestions were: Make RVers feel welcome with signs pertaining to RV parks and parking; make sure that law-enforcement officials are friendly and helpful; try to attract club rallies if there are facilities for such gatherings; and publicize special attractions and provide public parking areas designated for RVs near those special attractions.

I ended my speech with the admonition: Be kind to every RVer you meet. Who knows? When they hang up their keys, those folks might be your neighbors.

■ ■ ■

July 2000

Sn-o-o-o-ze

At a certain age, we reach what are sometimes called the Golden Years. From one who is there, let me tell you it isn't all gold. While many of the prevailing notions about older folks are true, in all fairness, some downsides should be noted. For example, it's undoubtedly true that the years bring more knowledge, more information filed away in the brain cells, but it's also a time when the old bod undergoes some changes that definitely aren't welcome either by you or those around you.

I'm a snorer, and as the years have passed my condition has gotten progressively worse. In fact, it got so bad that it was greatly disturbing Margie's sleep. At first, she coped with the problem by touching my face and telling me to roll over. I dutifully followed her instructions, and all was well for a while. But as the years went by, I developed another condition that aggravated an already exasperating situation—sleep apnea. I not only woke Margie up, but my periods of not breathing kept her awake and worried that I wouldn't wake up. Then I would snort loudly, not only reassuring her that I was alive, but waking myself up. So neither of us was getting unbroken sleep. Something had to be done.

Well, we took the obvious way out. Last winter, I started sleeping on the sofa in the living room of the motorhome and closed two doors between us. During the three or four months that we were at our home in Idaho, I used another bedroom—again with two closed doors between us. Although the arrangement worked as far as sleep was concerned, I still suffered from sleep apnea, which, I am informed, is a dangerous condition, and neither of us liked separate bedrooms.

During a routine physical examination last summer, I told our new primary-care doctor about the problem. It turned out that he has a great interest in sleep disorders and has become an expert on treatment. He recommended that I check into a sleep clinic at the local hospital for a study of my condition.

A couple of evenings later, I packed my pajamas and toothbrush and checked in at the hospital. Not knowing what to expect, I was a bit apprehensive. However, the nurse in charge of the examination soon allayed my fears with a detailed explanation, including a video, of what was coming up. Actually, it wasn't all that complicated. All I had to do was get ready for bed and jump in, and she hooked up what seemed like enough wiring to diagnose a faulty racing-car engine. The objective was to check all kinds of things relating to how I slept: inhaling, exhaling, oxygen intake, blood pressure, and a bunch of other things. I had been shown an example of how the measuring device worked, and I had concluded that it was a cross between an electrocardiogram and the seismograph that measures earthquakes.

I wasn't terribly uncomfortable. However, when the nurse pointed to a TV camera aimed directly at my bed and told me that she would be observing me all night, I began to have second thoughts. But it was too late to back out, so we said our goodnights, and I shut my eyes.

I slept well for a couple of hours, but was awakened by the nurse, who informed me that she was placing a face mask on me that she had previously explained was affixed to a continuous positive air pressure (CPAP) pump. Snoring and sleep apnea, she explained, were caused by a flap valve in my throat that jammed during my sleep. The mask she installed fed pressurized air directly into my nose through a plastic hose from the box-like pump (about the size of a small loaf of bread) on the bedside table. The only noise was the rush of air as it pushed into my nose. The purpose of the air pressure was to keep that flap open all the time, thereby stopping the snoring and keeping my breathing continuous. Surprisingly, I went back to sleep and slept perfectly until morning.

The next day, the nurse showed me all the monitoring gadgets. The real eye-opener was a rerun of the graph that showed my sleep pattern. Those zigzags on that graph for the first two hours of sleep clearly revealed how erratic my snoozing was. Zigzags showed rather normal inhaling and exhaling, followed by a flat line when I quit breathing, which was then followed by an enormous zigzag. That's when I caught my breath and snorted. But after the installation of the CPAP, the lines for the rest of the night were normal. Obviously the breathing device solved the problem.

The happy ending of the story is that I got one of those CPAP machines and have been using it for a year—in my own place in my own bed in my own bedroom. (When RVing, we have to be hooked up to shore power or use our inverter.)

In summary, that faint swishing of air lulls us both to sleep every night, putting another little chunk of gold in our Golden Years.

■ ■ ■

August 2000

Hills and Thrills

I just can't resist the lure of a road that we haven't been on before, and that's been the cause of some white-knuckle adventures for Margie—and even for me at times. Just a week ago when we were leaving Yuma, Arizona, for the Midwest, I plotted a new way to get to State Highway 89 between Congress and Prescott and State Highway 89A from Prescott to Cottonwood. And once again, I found myself on a narrow, steep, winding, hairpin-curve-laden road with Margie cringing in mortal fear as we wound our way up the sides of mountains with hundreds-of-foot drops on her side. To cap off the adventure, we had to go through downtown Jerome, a harrowing experience due to tourist traffic and an extremely narrow road, ending with a very steep downgrade. We both breathed a sigh of relief when the road flattened out at the base of the mountains.

On both highways, signs gave ample warning of road conditions ahead, but I simply refused to be intimidated by them. Since I have a Pacbrake on our 38-foot, 12-ton behemoth, I don't fear steep downhill grades, and with 300 Cummins horses, I don't worry about steep upgrades. Actually, the motorhome performs beautifully under those conditions; it's the people part of such audacious trip-planning that I must begin to pay more attention to. Perhaps my driving skills aren't what they used to be. Anyway, I'm going to think twice before I tackle that road again.

Our Arizona adventure brings to mind several other hill encounters over the years. We were Southern California residents when we started motorhoming, and since California has incredible mountains, it also has some incredibly hairy roads that lead to good fishing lakes and streams. At high elevations, pre-fuel-injection motorhomes frequently had problems on some of the steep hills 'way back in the boonies.

Being close to Nevada, we sometimes ventured north to the Reno–Lake Tahoe area. I recall vividly a time when I decided to take a shortcut from U.S. Highway 395 to South Lake Tahoe. According to the map that I look at now, it must have been State Highway 207 and what is called the Kingsberry Grade. Unfortunately, my 33-foot 1976 Foretravel with a Dodge 440 simply ran out of zip as we neared the top. Margie and I both were pushing on the dash trying to get over the hump, which we finally did.

Prior to the Foretravel, we had a 21-foot 1973 Shasta Class A with a Chevy 350. We took that little thing into places that would scare me to death today. I recall tackling 12,095-foot Independence Pass south of Aspen, Colorado, and having the engine vapor-lock somewhere near the top. In those days, I didn't get shook up by things like that. I simply pulled over and let the engine cool down, and then finished traversing the grade. In fact, the next day we took one of those roads marked UNPAVED from Silt to Vega Reservoir (look that one up on your map), where we enjoyed some great fishing right from our campsite.

Colorado has many great hills. State Highway 550 between Montrose and Durango is not for the faint-hearted. Red Mountain Pass is followed by Molas Divide and Coal Bank Hill Pass—all of which are in the 11,000-foot range. We did them in midsummer with a 36-foot Cross Country equipped with a Chevy 454 and didn't have a bit of trouble, but it was many exciting and carefully driven miles.

One of the worst stretches of highway I ever encountered was U.S. Highway 14A in Wyoming (Burgess Junction to Lovell). Believe me, if I ever again see a sign that says there is a 10 percent grade for ten miles, I'll pause and reconsider where I'm going. The Oh-My-God Hill has a name that is understandably earned. Even with a 300-hp diesel pushing us, we heated up and created more than a little concern before we topped out. I don't think I'll be going that way again.

But the absolute worst hill I ever encountered was on a road that leads out of Brian Head Ski Resort in Utah, just north of Cedar City. We wanted to see Cedar Breaks National Monument. We came in from the south on State Highway 148 and left on State Highway 143 to come out at Parowan. Right at the top of the hill was a sign warning that it was a 13 percent grade for thirteen miles. I tackled it anyway. I figured that by putting the Chevy 454 in first gear, I could hold the motorhome back. Oh, how mistaken I was. It didn't take long for the brakes to start smoking, but I managed to get stopped. After an hour's wait, l made it down alone (with Margie driving the dinghy) and a bit scared.

Yep, I've done some pretty good hills over the years. Obviously I haven't completely learned my lesson yet, but I don't think I'll be tackling any big ones for a while.

■ ■ ■

September 2000

Headin' South

I t's the time of year many motorhomers start thinking like ducks again—that is, thinking about headin' south. Real birds get the urge through some mysterious instinct; RV snowbirds get touched by the fever with the first sign of leaves turning gold. However, there's a big difference between our feathered friends and the people who travel in their wheeled homes. Nature's rules compel winged birds to return to the same roost by the same route year after year; people are free to make choices among many alternatives.

Despite the fact that many snowbirds return to the same nests year after year, more adventurous wheel-estate owners look at the big picture and experiment with different options in the Sun Belt. Although the basic ingredient that every snowbird seeks—warm weather—is present in most of the region from Florida to California, other factors lure large flocks to specific areas where havens for RVing snowbirds have been created. The major roosts are in Florida, Texas, and Arizona, and each has its special attractive features, as well as less desirable characteristics. Very simply, although all are wonderful, there is no perfect snowbird destination.

I have a few suggestions to offer snowbirds who are about to choose a winter roost.

- Go to a place where you already have friends. There's nothing better than having a pal show you the ropes in a new situation— introducing you to his or her friends, showing you where the best restaurants are, pointing out the local attractions and the best place to shop.

- Pay for only a couple of nights' visit while you scout out an area. If you like it, you can pay for more time; if not, you can pull up stakes.
- When you've found a place you like, pay by the month. The longer the period, the cheaper the rate. Parks that are $20 per night may be only $300 a month, which works out to only $10 a night. For someone who stays five months, the seasonal rate may be even better.
- If you have no strong preference (e.g., the dry climate of the Southwest as opposed to the humid climate of Florida), try out several places before you settle on one for regular wintering. Make a grand tour from Florida to California, and sample everything between.
- In snowbird parks, the variety of equipment and amenities may range from basic services to elegant, and you have to pay for the amenities whether or not you use them. If you don't use swimming pools, hot tubs, pool halls, or dance floors, there's no point in paying for them.
- Parks occupied primarily by park-model trailers generally aren't the best place for mobile people. Park-model folks tend to be less adventurous than those who travel extensively, and their interests tend to be more indoor- than outdoor-oriented. It isn't easy for short-term visitors to get into the swing of things with them.
- Condo parks (where you buy a site) can be a sensible solution if you know where you want to be for the long run, but it's not wise to buy before you do some experimenting. Most snowbirds eventually settle on an area to which they return year after year, and it may be wise to purchase your own spot once you have definitely selected your roost.
- Parks in major snowbird areas have the same people returning year after year and often are completely filled during peak winter

months. Many will not take short-term reservations, but it's a good idea to make reservations for January and February, if possible.

- If you have medical problems, check out the hospitals in the areas you are considering. It may be important to be close to one that specializes in a particular type of treatment. Not all snowbird areas have excellent medical facilities, but many have some of the best. For instance, a Mayo Clinic is located in Scottsdale, Arizona.
- Many motorhomers eat out a lot, so good restaurants are important to them. If you're fond of dining out, settling in for the winter where considerable driving is required to reach desirable restaurants might be unwise.
- Chambers of commerce or tourist bureaus can provide information about services available in a snowbird area. Most such agencies will furnish lists of all the local RV parks, restaurants, hospitals, and other services, as well as miscellaneous area information, including special attractions.

Choosing the place where you may be spending much of the rest of your life is an important decision, and should not be done without careful examination of all the available options. For the prospective snowbird, that means devoting several weeks or months to touring the Sun Belt, which means lots of miles and lots of places.

Life is hard indeed for a motorhomer!

■ ■ ■

October 2000

Making and
Keeping Extra Bucks

O ne reality of the early twenty-first century is that people live
     longer. Another is that some of the old ways of preparing
     for retirement may not work anymore. More years of living
means more money will be needed to live on for three, even four
decades of Golden Years. Consequently, baby boomers who are entering the ranks of retirees had better have bigger savings accounts, be prepared to extend their working years, or at least expect to make some
extra bucks with part-time work.

Not only will supplemental income be necessary to meet basic
expenses for some folks, but the fact that boomers have been accustomed to having more of the good things in life means that they will
expect more in their retirement years. The notion that when you retire
you will need only half as much income to live on no longer has validity. To the contrary, recent studies show that many retirees expect to
need as much income as they did before they retired.

Evidence of that kind of thinking is apparent with many of today's
motorhomers. Sales of motorhomes well in excess of $100,000 indicate
that some recent retirees have very expensive tastes in their rigs and their
lifestyles. An indication that some of them have miscalculated what their
retiree income requirements would be has been the tremendously
increased interest among RVers in earning money as they travel or, in
short, being "road workers."

Good news for road workers came early this year with the announce-
ment that the earnings ceiling for Social Security recipients has been

lowered to age sixty-five. Prior to that change in the law, wage-earners between the ages of sixty-five and seventy had to return a portion of their Social Security checks if they exceeded $17,000 in earned income and, like the income tax, the return increased as earnings increased. Consequently, many willing and able members of the labor pool chose to remain idle. Neither option was satisfactory nor fair.

It's a new ball game now for the thousands of RVers, particularly full-timers, who want to earn extra money. It's now possible for seniors over sixty-five to have their cake and eat it too. Some have to supplement their retirement incomes in order to maintain a lifestyle they prefer; some just want to be busy at something constructive. In most cases, the work is less than full time or is for intermittent stretches. However, others take on new careers with jobs that are for indefinite terms.

Not only has Uncle Sam given incentive to older folks to take employment by allowing them to keep more of what they earn, some employers look very favorably on that labor pool. Indeed, the assumption that retired people should be put out to pasture is fast losing ground. Many employers realize that the talents, experience, and work habits of older people can be a definite plus when it comes to filling some positions, so they directly solicit employees from the senior ranks. In snowbird areas, the winter influx of RV residents creates thousands of temporary jobs, particularly in the retail and service areas.

From the kinds of questions that I am frequently asked at seminar programs, I know that thousands of wannabe fulltimers are concerned about having enough income to support the lifestyle. I assure them that there are answers to their questions at the Life on Wheels conferences, held at colleges in Idaho, Pennsylvania, and Kentucky (see the Web site: lifeonwheels.com). In short, anyone who wishes to combine extended or full-time RVing and work can find ways to do so.

Most such people are interested in part-time employment and are not particularly concerned about workers' benefits such as health insurance, because they are covered by Medicare. However, as wage earners, they will pay into Social Security and, as a result, their benefits from that source will be increased every year that they pay into the system. If they take full-time employment with a company that offers health insurance, that insurance can be used as a supplement to Medicare, thereby eliminating that cost. A few companies offer such insurance to some categories of part-time employees.

Although most retirees in their early- to mid-sixties who take up RVing as a lifestyle are realizing a dream, many find that the habit of doing something useful is still with them even if they have no time clock to punch. Some take nonpaying jobs with volunteer organizations on a part-time basis; others begin whole new careers. It isn't unusual to learn that someone in his sixties has gone back to school to become a minister, a lawyer, or a teacher.

So, retirees over sixty-five, if it's work you want or need to make life complete, take comfort in the fact that many doors are open to you. And if you want more details on Social Security, call (800) 772-1213 or visit the Web site: ssa.gov.

■ ■ ■

December 2000

Update on Suzie

S orry, nonlovers of dogs, but this is going to be another one of those "I love my doggie" pieces that disgust those who don't understand the very special bonding that occurs between most dogs and their owners.

Although we used to take our family dog, Ginger, a shepherd-collie mix, with us on camping trips when the kids were young, Margie and I vowed never to have a dog or cat with us in the motorhomes in which we have spent much of the past quarter-century.

Watching other RVers having to structure their daily lives to accommodate their dogs convinced us that we definitely did not want our lives to be dictated by a pet. I always concluded my section on "taking pets" in my full-timing seminars with the declaration, "We will never have a dog as long as we are RVing." Regular readers know that I ate my words last year in my column "Never Say Never," as I reported how Suzie came into our lives.

Before I knew it as Suzie, a scruffy, dirty, grungy, pitiful-looking, obviously lost little dog started hanging around our parked motorhome at my sister's house in California. After shooing it away for three days, I relented and took it to a dog groomer, where I had it cleaned up and given a haircut. From there, it went to a vet for treatment of an infection. Then to the pet store for chow, leash, and rawhide bones. All this because I felt sorry for it. My plan was to find it a good home.

It was a nice little dog that apparently felt right at home with us in our motorhome. In fact, I think that in her mind, she had adopted us right off. We just didn't know it yet. After three or four days of caring

for her, we found someone who wanted a dog and we—a bit reluctantly—gave her up.

But that didn't work out. After three days, the new owner called and
asked to bring the dog back, complaining that it required too much
attention, and we ended up with something we said we would never
have. But I have to admit that it is the best thing that has happened to
us in many years. Suzie has been the most delightful addition to our
family since the last grandchild was born.

Suzie is a born traveler. All we have to do is open the motorhome door,
and she's ready to roll. Watching out the window for cows and horses,
which she loves to bark at from the safety of the motorhome, she sits
with Margie, either on her lap or squeezed into the seat beside her.

Fortunately for us, Suzie was already housebroken and she understands basic commands. Since she seems to be so at home in the motorhome, we speculate that she could even have belonged to a motorhome
family.

As for her ancestry, we are still in a quandary. I've been informed
by several apparently knowledgeable dog owners that she is this or that.
My best guess is that she is an AKA-registered Heinz 57. I haven't really
tried to find out because it doesn't make any difference. I just know that
she's my dog.

Suzie's attention-getter when she wants something is to stand on her
hind legs and paw the air as she stares you right in the eye. She uses it
when she wants to go out, get a treat, or take a walk. How can anyone
ignore a dog that is dancing around on its hind legs and staring at you?
I usually figure out what she wants and do it. She got my number real
early in this game and has me well trained.

Besides being the little charmer that she is, Suzie is good for my
health. We start out our mornings with a walk, and we end the day
the same way. As a zipper-club member, I have instructions to walk at

least two miles a day, and Suzie makes those health treatments especially pleasant.

As a longtime critic of bad dog owners, those who feel that pet rules in parks and other public places were written for other people, I have tried to be especially careful to obey the rules wherever we are. Fortunately, Suzie is not a barker, so we don't have to worry about that. Also, when we have to leave her in the motorhome (not outside) while we do something, we check on her at least every two hours—and we make sure she always has the right amount of food and fresh water.

Suzie loves people, which is fortunate because we are so often with others, and many of them love her. One lady makes homemade treats for her and even sent some while we were on the road last winter. Another lady made her a special sleeping rug. When we attend functions like the Life on Wheels programs, people we've never met ask about her.

The medical experts say that older people who have pets are happier, healthier, more mentally alert, and live longer than those who don't. I know that Suzie is making the first three work for us. We're hoping Number 4 works, too.

■ ■ ■

January 2001

Walking

S even years ago, my chest was carved open and my heart taken out for some plumbing repairs. To keep from having a repeat performance, my doctor urged me to exercise regularly to help keep the pipes flushed. Among his recommendations was that I take brisk walks at least three times weekly.

I like walking. It gives me an opportunity to see things at close range. And it gives me "think time." This morning, during my regular two-mile hike, I came up with the idea for this column. With my buddy Suzie trotting along beside me, I let my brain wander. Whether it's about writing, Life on Wheels conferences, repairing the motorhome, or my kids and grandkids, I find that brisk striding stimulates my thinking processes. Often I find answers to my questions as I improve my physical well-being.

Since we are in so many different places during a typical year, I get to experience a variety of walkways. In most RV parks, a walk usually consists of several times around the perimeter of the park—or going up and down the rows. Unfortunately from the health-benefit standpoint, I often stop to gab with fellow RVers, which slows down the heart rate that the walk is supposed to stimulate. Walks in public parks are usually the best kind, simply because they are located in beautiful places with interesting things to see. Indeed, a long hike in a national park is easy-to-take medicine.

One of my favorite RV parks for walking is Country Roads (a condo resort) in Yuma, Arizona. We spent some winters there in the mid-1980s and developed a habit of starting every morning with a brisk promenade around the two-mile perimeter. In the years since, we have made stops there for brief periods every winter and we always enjoy the walks, just as we did years ago (they're a bit slower now, though).

Another regular stop on our winter circuit is at my sister's house in San Dimas, California, where we park a few blocks from the middle of town. It's a different kind of walk, since it's all on city sidewalks, but I enjoy looking at people's houses and lawns. San Dimas is a quaint town with a lot of city pride. All of the old business section has been renovated with a Western motif—boardwalks, false fronts, and antique shops with lots of old stuff out front. I usually include the three blocks of the main part of town in my circuit.

When we are at home in Idaho, my daily walks vary little, but are always interesting. Since our land includes the entry road to a national forest, the setting is much like that of a beautiful park. Almost invariably, we see some wildlife—elk, deer, wild turkeys, squirrels, owls, hawks, grouse, pheasants, maybe even a bear—on our two-mile hike on the dirt road that wends its way through the woods. I even enjoy looking at the trees, especially the incredibly straight white firs that stretch ever so far up to reach the sunlight. But my favorite tree is a huge cedar, the biggest tree in that part of the forest. Not only is my forest walk good for jazzing up my circulation, it also soothes the mind.

We are always in Illinois in early September for Margie's mother's birthday (101 this year). Our motorhome parking place is under a big maple tree in the yard of the house where I grew up. My brother owns it now, and his hospitality includes full hookups. Although I enjoy my walks wherever they are, the one I enjoy most is the route I took this morning—a mile up a country road to the one-room schoolhouse where I learned readin', 'ritin' and 'rithmetic. At this time of year (September), the tall corn on both sides of the road is turning brown, and there's a bit of a nip in the air as the sun rises.

When I was a boy, I walked that road for eight years, so I knew who lived in all the houses that I passed. Back then, kids came from all of them and joined the Maxwell kids as we trudged that long, graveled mile. Now those houses are occupied by the children and/or grand-children of those who owned them in my childhood, and the road is paved. In my mind, I can still see those kids and their now-gone par-ents. The old one-room schoolhouse still stands, kept in good repair by the folks who use it for community get-togethers. The pump at the well still works, so Suzie can quench her thirst; she covers about three lop-ing miles to my single one. I look forward to taking that walk for many more years.

Although my walks are required as part of the program for keep-ing my old ticker ticking, I don't look at them as medicine. We can cover a lot of miles in our marvelous machines and get to a lot of fabulous places. But only by walking can you really see the little things that make up this big wonderful world. And, as a special bonus, it gives you the opportunity to exercise your brain cells as well as your muscles.

■ ■ ■

March 2003

Goin' Home

I t's getting to be that time of the year when snowbirds in Florida, Texas, Arizona, and many lesser gathering spots in the south are beginning to think "North." And in most cases, that means heading home. For many motorhomers that home is simply another RV park, but for most it means a conventional abode of one kind or another—a house, an apartment, a condo, or a mobile home. In all cases, it means following the sun as the Earth's axis tilts ever so slowly to focus its beams on higher latitudes.

Fulltimers may have two parks that they consider home bases, so they go home twice each year, but never change the way they live the way regular homeowners do. As might be expected, the northern base is often close to relatives, especially the kids. The summer months are a time for catching up with not only offspring, but brothers, sisters, aunts, uncles, and, especially, grandkids. In fact, summer camping spaces may simply be the driveways of relatives and friends. Summers are filled with family fun without all the work that a house entails. But as the summer wanes and the leaves start to change color, thoughts of favorite southern homes begin to loom large. And by the time the first frost hits, many fulltimers are already on roads marked SOUTH, where they will often join their RVing "families" for a few months of a different kind of fun.

Although fulltiming has an abundance of practitioners and even more wannabes, most snowbirds still own conventional homes. They want to escape cold winters where those homes are located, but they don't want to give up entirely the lifestyle they have become accustomed to. So they look to their RVs as a means of escape during the winter months. It's interesting how those folks are able to rearrange and adjust their way of life so quickly—usually twice a year. Like birds, the urge to move possesses them twice annually and they have to give in to it. And usually it's to the same places both times.

If it weren't for the importance to most people of having tangible roots somewhere, the number of totally mobile snowbirds would be more than our highways could accommodate. Judging from the number of RVers who attend seminars on fulltiming at RV shows and rallies, interest in that lifestyle is enormous. However, many of those folks prefer to be "fulltimers" only part of the year. They want to have their cake—albeit a smaller piece—and eat it too. The concept of a conventional home is so firmly ingrained in people that it is unlikely we will ever see a time when most snowbirds are fulltimers. So the northern-home/southern-home cycle will likely continue in the foreseeable future, as it is now.

In my seminars on fulltiming, I always explain up front that there's nothing wrong in not wanting to give up one's regular home. Not everyone is cut out to live entirely on wheels. In fact, I point out that although Margie and I spend most of our time in our motorhome, we still maintain a regular home in Idaho. And we are like old horses who smell the barn when the sap starts running in the springtime. Although we are perfectly happy in our motorhome wherever we happen to be, there comes a time every year when we want to go home.

There are some great benefits in keeping a regular home even though you expect to be spending much of your time in a motorhome. It's the only way to keep all of your things where you can enjoy them when you want to. No matter how many experts say that things don't really matter, there are many people who don't agree. They want their belongings, including a house, so they will never be happy as fulltimers. But those who live in northern climes are perfectly willing to forsake those things every winter in exchange for places where cold days are in the mid-sixties.

For most snowbirds who keep their houses, the chief drawback is economic. Very simply, you can leave a house, but you can't leave the cost of owning it. You may live in it only half the time, but you will pay taxes, insurance, and maintenance full time. Property also involves a lot of catch-up work when you arrive home in the spring. In fact, following the surge of exultation we experience after turning into the tree-lined lane that leads to our house, we find that the joy of homecoming is somewhat dampened when we see the work that needs to be done, inside and out. I'm sure that we, like many other motorhomers, will see the time when we will opt for a simpler northern abode, but that time isn't here yet.

For over two decades, we have been snowbirds with two homes. One has wheels, the other one doesn't. We gladly roll out of the driveway at our house every autumn; we gladly return to it in the spring. We're on our way as I am writing this month's column. It feels good to be goin' home.

■ ■ ■

April 2001

On Balance

B alance is normal. It's amazing how many aspects of our lives reflect both high points and low points. A lot of good things happen, but sometimes we must endure the bad. We work; we play. Our pace is sometimes frantic; at other times, we loaf. Motorhomers are particularly fortunate in that we have the wheels to take us to see the places and do the things that give us pleasure. But, of course, we have those great times balanced with those things that definitely are not fun—motorhome problems, less-than-desirable campgrounds, bad weather, and, nowadays, high fuel prices. But that's the way life is. We have to learn to accept the downs that go along with the ups.

One of the great joys of family life is the birth of a child. Our children, our grandchildren, and, eventually, our great-grandchildren delight us with the perpetuation of ourselves in the genes they inherit from us. Unfortunately, the reality is that as new ones take their places in our lives, old ones inevitably leave. And the older we get, the more we experience those sad events. The joy at the birth of new ones never diminishes, nor does the sorrow of the leaving of old ones. But it's a balancing act that we simply have to accept.

Like most people of our age, our parents grew old, became ill, and have passed on over the years. Regular readers of this column may recall that, for over a decade, Margie and I have geared our travels to extended visits with her mother in a long-term care facility in Illinois. At age 101, she passed away last November. Luke, our first great-grandchild, was born a week later. Clearly that is an example of balance in our lives.

I had the privilege of knowing and enjoying the company of Margie's mother for more than fifty years. She was the perfect mother-in-law.

Although we lived 2,000 miles apart, she always made an extended and very welcome visit to our house every year. Consequently, she was quite influential in our children's lives. Her gentle, loving nature, kindness, and willingness to help with any work that needed to be done were positive examples for all of us. As Margie and I struggled with the problems of making a living and raising kids, she was a stabilizing influence when she was with us. We did appreciate her help when we needed it; I know she appreciated our visits with her, particularly Margie's loving care, when she could no longer manage on her own. I know there's some balance there. But we will always remember and miss her.

Little Luke is with us now. We changed our lifestyle pattern just for his arrival to enable us to enjoy this newest family member. Last summer, his mother (our granddaughter) asked if we would stay home until after Christmas so she could be with us for the month of December. Although we knew that we would be confronted with weather conditions quite a bit different from our normal winters in Arizona, Florida, and California, we didn't hesitate to agree to stay in Idaho.

Indeed, as I write this, I can look out the window at well over two feet of snow, and it is still coming down. The thermometer is reading in the low 'teens. It's definitely not what we are accustomed to at this time of the year. But I can look over toward the fireplace and see my granddaughter feeding that tiny, very hungry, little fellow, and I don't mind this temporary lifestyle change at all. We may have to put up with a bit of nasty weather, but the joy of having our great-grandson with us for the first few weeks of his life is a trade-off that we will cherish forever. And for the first time in fourteen years, we'll have kids and grandkids with us for Christmas. These things definitely tilt the scales in favor of the pluses in life.

I think most of us realize that we don't live in a perfect world and that things are going to happen that we wish didn't. And most of us successfully cope with whatever problems come along. If we don't learn to deal positively with those problems, we lose the balance that is so crucial for a good life. One of life's biggest lessons is learning to accept what is inevitable. That, of course, includes the aging process and the eventual passing of our loved ones.

Unfortunately, a few motorhomers focus on the bad incidents of this lifestyle, the mostly minor calamities that are simply part of the game. Those folks either forget or ignore all the times their rigs functioned perfectly, the roads were excellent, the campgrounds were great, people were wonderful, and the sights magnificent. It is regrettable that there is a downside in this lifestyle, just as there is a downside in almost everything. But we must not let that dominate our thinking and our behavior. We should always be aware of the good side and let it tilt the scales to the positive side of the way we live.

On balance, life is good.

■ ■ ■

May 2001
It Doesn't Matter

H ow much easier life would be for most of us if we would only realize that "Whatever you think matters—doesn't." Not only would it make life more pleasant, but it would add years to our life spans. That's according to Roger Rosenblatt in his wonderful new book, *Rules for Aging*, in which he claims that if you "resist every normal impulse, a perfect life is yours forever."

I first learned of Rosenblatt's book in a *Time* magazine article, in which excerpts from his book outlined a philosophy laced with great wit and wisdom. I was wowed by Rule Number One, which was quoted in its entirety in the review. According to that rule, all of the concerns that cause us anguish and worry should be totally ignored. Some tongue-in-cheek elaboration on that rule, with a listing of things that we might think matter, provides food for serious thought. In fact, in our household (motorhomehold?), it has become a comeback for all the minor disagreements and doubts that plague our normal lives. When we find ourselves involved in those questions and disputes, someone invariably quips, "It doesn't matter," and in most cases, we laugh the issue away.

Of course, I'm not suggesting that Rosenblatt's philosophy is intended to be all-inclusive about the things we think about and the issues we face, but each of his humorous rules has a kernel of truth imbedded in it. I think all of us could benefit by adhering to Rule Number One in so many of the instances in which we overreact mentally (sometimes physically) to issues that, if thought about seriously, really aren't that important. Many of the anxieties, arguments, blaming, fussing—and sometimes fighting—that we burden our lives with could be dismissed with the simple declaration, "It doesn't matter."

Since I'm writing this on New Year's Day, it is the perfect time for reflection on some of the things that upset or worried me in the past year. For my own benefit (and perhaps yours), I'm going to review some of those that make me cringe when I look back at the times when I should have said to myself, "It doesn't matter."

It seems that I always manage to choose lines in grocery stores composed of people who piddle around writing checks (why don't they fill out everything but the amount while waiting for the groceries to be checked?) or who wait until the last item has been rung up and checked and then start digging in their purses for the money, including digging in their change pockets for the exact penny. I often, in an effort to distract myself from the situation, read whole issues of the *National Enquirer* while waiting for those poky people to get moving.

When on the road, it seems that I always have to wait to register at campgrounds behind a half-dozen other RVers who have chosen the same campground I have just before I got there. Like an old horse smelling the barn, I'm anxious to get to my stall and get settled for the evening (and get my attitude adjusted), but I'm forced to wait impatiently for my turn, hoping that one of those ahead of me doesn't take the last space. (I've had it happen!)

Then there are the disagreements that cause Margie and me sometimes to get our hackles up—like whether to leave on a big trip on Friday or Saturday, whether we should take this or that with us, whether one of us said this or said that, whether we should buy this or that, or whose fault it was that I forgot something, and so on—major issues that deserve much attention and definitely are worth quarreling over!

I have more than a fair share of looking back at things that I should have said, or should not have said, at some of the public appearances I have made in the past year, or in conversations with various people. I just know that I offended some, or that they misinterpreted me because I wasn't clear enough in my explanation of whatever my point was. Oh, how I regret that I can't say some things over again.

I recall very distinctly remarking to Margie a year ago, when the stock market was sky-high, that maybe we should sell every stock and put the cash in CDs. But I didn't, because I thought that the market would go even higher. It bothers me now when I think that if I had only followed my gut, we would be a heck of a lot better off financially.

But after reading Roger Rosenblatt's book, I've decided to take his advice about some of the things that I've fussed about in the past. All fifty-eight of his rules are worth careful consideration, and it may be practical, as the author suggests, to commit them to memory. For sure, I am indelibly printing Rule Number One on the front of my brain for quick resurrection when those occasions arise that might ruffle my feathers or otherwise cause me to be disturbed or anxious.

It doesn't matter.

■ ■ ■

July 2001

RV Care-A-Vanners

Some folks say that charity begins at home; another very special group says that charity begins with building a home. That's the creed of the RV Care-A-Vanners, a volunteer group of RVers affiliated with Habitat for Humanity. Mixing RVing and nail-pounding, they travel around the country, applying their labors to the construction of homes for the less fortunate.

An example of the do-gooding of these generous, hard-working people was on display at the recent Great North American RV Rally in Perry, Georgia. Situated inside the gate at the fairground was a just-completed 1,100-square-foot three-bedroom house. It had been built in ten working days by twenty unpaid volunteer couples who are members of the RV Care-A-Vanners.

A branch of Habitat for Humanity International, an organization dedicated to eliminating poverty housing worldwide and made famous by its most illustrious volunteer, former President Jimmy Carter, RV Care-A-Vanners are RVers who dedicate periods of time to helping with the program. Coming from all walks of life, all ages, all occupations, all skill levels, RV Care-A-Vanners must meet only two requirements: have an RV in which to live and, of course, be willing to work.

Although approximately half the volunteers have skills in some aspects of house-building, that isn't a requirement for membership; many of the other half have never seriously used a hammer or a saw. Under the tutelage of a supervisor, they soon master enough carpentry skills to be useful. Even the "boss" at the Perry job was not a construction specialist. Indeed, Paul Casilli's regular job, from which he was taking a vacation to supervise the construction of the house on the fair-grounds, is in the computer business.

Although relatively small, the homes are a giant step up in housing for the lucky recipients. The one built by the RV Care-A-Vanners at Perry was being moved only a mile and a half away for permanent installation, to be occupied by a single mother and her two children who would, for the first time, experience the joy of living in a brand-new house at a price and terms she could afford.

The houses aren't free. Recipients must put in 500 hours of "sweat equity" either in the house they are to receive or in another being built for someone else. The lady who was to receive the Perry house worked on her house every day. Also, a purchase price commensurate with the income of the recipient family is set, and no-interest payments are made on the mortgage.

RV Care-A-Vanners, who number approximately 2,000 (600 active at one time), build sixty houses a year. When affiliates of the national organization elect to do a "build," they put in a call to headquarters, and volunteers from the club are invited via the club's quarterly newsletter to participate. Ten or twelve couples are selected for each job.

Materials for the houses are obtained in various ways, some by dona-tions in materials and some by cash contributions. Some large com-panies commit to long-term participation; Whirlpool Corporation, for example, provides all the appliances for many of the houses. The mate-rials for the house at Perry were paid for by the rally attendees; read-ers of *MotorHome, Trailer Life, Coast to Coast,* Good Sam's *Highways,* and Woodall's publications; and a gift from their parent company, Affin-ity Group Inc. The land on which Habitat houses are placed is often donated by companies or individuals.

RV Care-A-Vanner builds are coordinated by Habitat for Humanity International headquarters. Local affiliates of the Habitat organization arrange for a caravan of ten or twelve couples to meet at a site where a house is to be constructed. The volunteers must provide their own housing, living expenses, and tools, although they are provided with a safe place to park their rigs. Sometimes they stay at a church parking lot or, in some cases, in spaces donated by a generous campground owner.

RV Care-A-Vanners was founded twelve years ago by Jack and Lois Wolters, an RVing couple who wanted to make a contribution to the ideals of Habitat for Humanity. By word-of-mouth, the club has grown to its present size, and hundreds of houses have been built by its members.

Spokesperson Marge Kitterman said, "We get a lot more out of it than we put in, and that's the feeling of doing something worthwhile while enjoying RVing."

Now, that's a philosophy that I can relate to.

To obtain information regarding how to participate in the RV Care-A-Vanners, upcoming caravan dates, and locations, call (800) HABI-TAT, ext. 2446, or check out the Web site: habitat.org. E-mail can be sent to rvinfodesk@hfhi.org; snail mail to: RV Care-A-Vanners Information Desk, 121 Habitat Street, Americus, Georgia 31709.

■ ■ ■

August 2001
Smaller Is Better

O ne has only to attend any gathering of motorhomers to understand that the slogan "bigger is better" has been the key to motorhome buying in the 1990s. The "big" 33-footers of the 1970s and 1980s became "little" in the just-passed decade as thousands of buyers opted for rolling homes in the 40-foot range. In fact, even larger rigs—42- to 45-footers—found favor with high-line buyers. And diesel engines were the power choice for those folks. Indeed, the "bigger is better" slogan applied to those engines too, as horsepower shot up in direct proportion to coach length. Keeping up with the Joneses meant big diesel pushers with lots of horses.

While this trend in motorhomes was very apparent, a subtle trend in the opposite direction began for fifth-wheels in the mid-1990s. As slideouts became larger and more popular, fiver owners began to downsize and opted for rigs in the 30- to 35-foot range. They discovered that three slideouts allowed for living comfort without the problems that come with longer rigs. That same kind of thinking is now becoming popular among motorhome buyers, and the industry is accommodating them. One has only to look at the offerings of the major motorhome manufacturers to see that most of them are catering to the "smaller is better" philosophy.

There is little actual difference in living space between a nonslideout 40-foot motorhome and a 32-footer with two slideouts. The former has approximately 340 square feet of floor space to begin with, but well over half is covered with cabinets, closets, a bed, bathroom facilities, kitchen appliances, seating, and a driving area. The actual free floor space in most motorhomes is a 3-foot-wide (or less) aisle that runs from front to rear. In a slideout model, what appears to be vast floor space is opened up while preserving storage and cabinet capability. In fact, with a large slideout in the living area and a smaller one in the bedroom, a 32-footer has well over 300 square feet of floor. Although floor space is comparable in a nonslide 40-footer and a 32-footer with three slides, two important factors favor the shorter unit: (1) 8 feet less in length means a lot when it comes to jockeying into a campground space, maneuvering in traffic, or trying to find a parking space; and (2) the living space is more livable. An opened-up living–dining room allows people to sit opposite each other without knocking knees or, in my case, having my chair at my computer desk blocking the aisle. Bedroom configurations utilizing the slideout usually include a slideout clothes closet or a bed slideout that leaves plenty of room for a vanity/closet area at the foot of the bed.

I saw a more extreme example of motorhome downsizing while retaining a considerable degree of livability at the Great North American RV Rally at Perry, Georgia. Coachmen's Aurora was displayed in a 26-foot model with a large slideout in the living–dining area. It was a great solution for someone who prefers a short rig that retains some of the livability features of larger models. The Allegro 30-footer with a slideout is Tiffin Motor Homes' bestseller, and their popular new 26-foot model with a bedroom slideout is relatively roomy. For those who prefer diesel, a 32-foot Allegro diesel pusher with a slideout will be on the market soon. Winnebago's 26-footer has long been a staple in their product line in both Brave and Sunrise (Itasca) versions, but neither presently offers slideouts.

Although most of us who spend a great deal of our time in our motorhomes will stick with big ones, there is definitely a place for smaller rigs. Nearly all of us, at some point, will change our lifestyle patterns, either by necessity or choice. Maybe that change will involve cutting back in the amount of time spent in the motorhome, so a smaller one will become more practical both in terms of ease of operation and in economy.

For example, once-avid motorhomers by the thousands have at a certain stage of their lives opted for park models in RV parks for their primary RV abode, but they still want a motorhome for side trips and going to and from their house in the north. Others don't feel comfortable driving a large rig anymore, but still want to travel even if it means forsaking some interior coach space.

The economic factor is also a very good reason for buying a small rig. Not only does it cost less to purchase, it also is probably more economical to operate. With fuel costs escalating as they are, that can become an even more significant factor in the future. In short, shorter is cheaper.

No doubt about it, the slideout has been the most significant change in motorhome design since self-containment. In fact, there seems to be a race to see who can include the most slideouts in a floorplan. As with fifth-wheels, three slideouts on motorhomes are becoming more popular. That third slide adds up to eight more feet of floor space, which makes the kitchen–dining–living area very spacious. In fact, I've seen a few of the huge bus conversions with four slides.

I wonder what company will come up with a slideup that will create an upstairs or a slideback that will stretch out the back end of a motorhome. Heck, maybe even a slidedown that will make a basement. I'm sure that if they're built, some of us will buy them.

■ ■ ■

September 2001

Campgrounds and Apples

I've often heard that 5 percent of any classification of people consists of really bad apples: hypocritical preachers, dumb teachers, shyster lawyers, crooked businessmen, cheating card players, mean mothers, drunken fathers, incompetent employees, and so on. And as with all other groups, the fact that there are some bad apples among RVers is undeniable. One can argue only about the actual percentage who fit in that category.

A few months ago, Tom Gonser, who manages the great Web site rversonline.com, attended a National Association of RV Parks and Campgrounds convention, during which he surveyed the group about troublesome issues with customers. Although Gonser emphasizes that his survey is not highly scientific, the results clearly indicate that the bad apples among us definitely make an impression on those who provide the accommodations for us during our travels. Unfortunately those of us who try to be model customers are lumped in with our disgraceful brethren in the views of some campground owners.

Not picking up after their dogs is ranked the number one complaint, and barking dogs is number two. One would think, after all the controversy about dogs in campgrounds that flares up regularly, that this issue would have been laid to rest long ago. Obviously, it hasn't, which indicates that bad dog owners are still all too prevalent in campgrounds. As a considerate dog owner myself, I regret that I might be lumped into the category of those who have no respect for normal campground rules. Very simply, people who won't pick up after their dogs or who allow their dogs to bark in campgrounds don't deserve those pets—and don't deserve to be served by campground owners.

Number 3 on the list of troublesome customer issues reported by campground owners is speeding. Not only is that issue one of consideration for fellow campers, but it very much concerns safety. In campgrounds with lots of children, speeding is particularly dangerous. Kids let loose after a day of travel tend to be active and, in the confines of a busy campground, can pop out from behind an RV almost instantly. A vehicle going 20 mph in that situation can be a serious threat to those children. And, since most campgrounds have low speed limits posted (usually 10 mph maximum), there are serious legal ramifications for speeders who are involved in accidents in campgrounds.

Kids aren't the only group threatened by speeders in RV parks. In snowbird areas, nearly all RV park residents are retirees. Not as agile as they once were, these folks are definitely threatened by speeders.

Improper parking of vehicles rated fourth among campground owners' problems with customers. The inconsiderate customer parks his truck or car where it shouldn't be (for example, on the grass or blocking traffic). From a personal standpoint, I can recall instances where a vehicle parked in front of an RV across a narrow road from my site made it difficult or impossible to make the turn when I was ready to leave in the morning. Often the only reason those vehicles are parked where they are is so the owner will be a few steps closer to his RV entry door. A considerate camper takes note of how his neighbors will be affected by his parked vehicles.

Amazing as it may seem, trashing facilities is a big problem in many campgrounds. Although usually caused by young people who tear things up simply for the joy of doing so, sometimes careless, inconsiderate older folks leave messes in restrooms that they wouldn't at home or in their RVs. Campgrounds that are near popular family attractions bear the brunt of such problems. The basic cause actually is inconsiderate parents who don't properly supervise their children.

Among other customer problems cited by campground owners were some that portray RVers as cheapskates. Included in that category were "no-shows" and "dishonest claim of number of persons or pets." During peak seasons, when parks are operating at maximum capacity, no-shows create problems both for the campground owners who lose money if they haven't collected payment in advance and for other RVers who would have used those spaces had they been available. Under-reporting the number of people or pets at registration time is simply lying and cheating. Obviously people who do that lack character.

Gonser's survey clearly indicates that among RVers as a group, we have our percentage of bad apples. As with most groups, there's not much the 95 percent of us who try to do things right can do to change the 5 percent who do things wrong. However, we can always go that extra mile to create the impression that, as a group, all RVers haven't been spoiled by those few rotten apples in the bottom of the barrel.

■ ■ ■

October 2001

The Good Old Days?

O ne of the banes of extended RVing is getting personal services that meet your standards. Particularly annoying to me is the problem of getting an acceptable haircut in a strange shop. I'm not unusually finicky, but I've had some awful experiences over the years. I've been skinned, chopped, nicked, crowned, and overcharged.

Consequently, I solved the problem a number of years ago by establishing a chain of reliable hair-cutters around the country at places we usually visit every year. There's Patti in Illinois, Don (the Bushwhacker) in Arizona, Shawn in California, and Heather in Idaho. They're all good at their trade, and I have no fears when I sit down in their chairs.

I'm a bit partial to Heather, though. She's a cutie in her mid-twenties, and, according to Margie, she gives me the best haircut of all. She clips me more often than the others because she's in Idaho where we spend our summers at home. Not only is she an excellent hair-cutter, she comes to our house to do the clipping. On warm days, we put up a stool out on the deck and she clips and snips while I admire the beauty of the countryside. And for icing on the cake, she doesn't charge me anything and even gives me a peck on the cheek when she's done. How's that for service? Incidentally, Heather is my granddaughter and owns her own beauty shop in Coeur d'Alene.

Sometimes when I'm getting a haircut, I think of my worst experience in that department, as one of five boys (and four girls) in a struggling family in Illinois during the 1930s. My mother did the hair-cutting. Even though a store-bought haircut was only a quarter, we couldn't afford it. Not only were we very poor (although we weren't aware of it), the rural electrification program had not reached our area, so Mom's clippers were hand-operated. I'm sure she had pretty good arm muscles, but her hands must have gotten awfully tired by the time she got through with all five boys. I know she got impatient with our squirming, protesting, and sometimes bawling, and that caused her to jerk and pull our hair as she worked the clippers. Of all Mom's virtues, and there were many (she was a saint), painless hair-cutting was not one of them.

At our house, haircut day was an ordeal for everyone involved. In fact, we sometimes had to be rounded up from various hiding places to take our places on what was to us something akin to the electric chair. I know Mom didn't enjoy the chore either, but, like most of the trials and tribulations of the day, she simply did what had to be done. Her boys might look a bit nicked up after her handiwork, but we weren't shaggy-looking.

Margie hasn't been quite as successful as I have in locating beauticians who can properly deal with her very fine hair. Heather knows how to deal with it, and although she has given her Grammie very specific instructions to pass on to other beauticians who do her hair, it seldom works out exactly right. The result has often left Margie very unhappy after visits to unfamiliar hair salons. Since we plan to spend several winter months in Yuma, where she had a very unsatisfactory experience last year, she will be faced with trying someone new again.

Handling medical problems on the road used to be very difficult. Situations requiring a doctor meant either going to a hospital emergency room or calling doctors' offices to find one that would take you right away. Having prescriptions written in advance by one's regular doctor was the only way to buy medicines while away from home without the expense and trouble of being diagnosed by a new doctor. Nowadays both of those problems are nonexistent. They have been solved by walk-in clinics and Wal-Mart pharmacies. Last winter, for example, I got an ear infection in Yuma. Not only was I able to get in right away at one of those clinics, but the doctor who treated me gave me a prescription and recommended that I get it filled across the border in Algodones, Mexico. Great service without hassle and an apparent concern with the cost of the rather expensive medicine!

Life on the road isn't always perfect. Anyone who has been at it for a while knows that we have to put up with some less-than-ideal circumstances at times. However, when you take a look at the big picture and compare what we have now with what we had to cope with in the past, we have to admit that we've got it pretty darn good right now.

And when I think I'm having a hard time with haircuts nowadays, all I have to do is think of those days a long time ago when a session with Mom the Barber was really something to get upset about. The reality is that a few days' growth will obliterate the signs of any botched job. That's the way it is with most of our problems.

In fact, we should realize that the good old days are here and now.

■ ■ ■

November 2001

Copper Canyon Caravan

C opper Canyon! Piggyback! Bigger than Grand Canyon! I'd heard the hoopla about this allegedly fantastic trip to mainland Mexico for two decades. At last, I've "been there, done that" and found that it was all that it was purported to be.

Actually a series of deep valleys, the Copper Canyon stretches for days of very unhurried travel (average speed 18 mph). How many miles I don't know but it seemed like hundreds. Many of the small villages we saw were connected only by primitive dirt roads, and 1 would guess that most inhabitants seldom if ever see real towns. Indeed many of the Tarahumara Indians who fled from the Spaniards to these almost impenetrable mountains hundreds of years ago cultivated tiny mountainside farms, so isolated that their inhabitants possibly never saw what we refer to as civilization.

Our guide at Divisidero informed us that many of the colorfully costumed Tarahumara women who weave and sell baskets climb for hours every day to peddle their wares where the tourist trains stop. Not only do they have to carry their baskets, but most of them bring small children. However, their treks bring results; few tourists can resist buying some of the beautiful baskets for a few pesos. I thought Margie went overboard with thirteen, but my sister bought closer to fifty.

Incredibly, there is a first-class hotel at the top of Copper Canyon. A bus took us from Divisidero via an unbelievably bumpy dirt road to a castlelike structure perched on a mountainside, where we were wined and dined in splendor.

After five days in our motorhome atop a railroad flatcar, we again took to the roads. We visited Los Mochis (where we unloaded from rail cars and later enjoyed Las Glorias beach camping); La Fuerte (wonderful hotel dining experience and a tour of a government building); Mazatlan (shopping fishing, sightseeing, and all sorts of touristy things); and San Carlos (excellent RV park, great fishing, super dining, and a tour of a pearl farm). Every city has something special to offer.

Among the small towns and villages, Copala and Alamos are by far our favorites. Although different in many respects, both are former silver-mining towns that were exploited by the Spaniards, and both are accessible by less-than-perfect roads. Copala is quite small, but boasts a wonderful restaurant, Daniel's, where we topped off our traditional Mexican lunch with the restaurant's special dessert: a banana coconut-cream pie. Go figure!

Alamos has been modernized, due in part to an influx of permanent residents from the United States and Canada. Some of the old homes have been restored with modern amenities. The plaza that fronts a picture-book cathedral bustled with both locals and tourists.

Caravans are a great way to explore Mexico for those who have some trepidation about travel in that country or who prefer to have someone one else do all the planning. Not only do caravans provide the security of numbers, but wagon masters do all the dirty work. Knowing where to find the special places and important things is so important to travelers in foreign places. Caravans provide that service

Although Mexican roads earned a bad name in the past, that isn't the case nowadays. There still are some bad roads (as in the United States), but the main roads, particularly the toll roads, are quite good. Incidentally, toll fees mount up; more than $260 for our twenty-three-day trip. Fuel, although relatively expensive, is readily available at the ubiquitous Pemex stations. Most gas stations present no access problems for big motorhomes.

Of course, we had heard horror stories about crime in Mexico, but fear of *banditos* was never an issue with us. Two *federales* accompanied us while on the train, and we did not wander around on darkened streets. In fact, we felt more welcomed by the people we met in Mexico than we often do upon encountering strangers in the United States. The reality is that the crime rate in Mexico is much lower than it is in our country.

Although a Copper Canyon caravan trip has its great moments and gives a group of RVers opportunities to create new friendships, participants sometimes have to tolerate less-than-perfect weather conditions, as with most RV trips. The mountains of Copper Canyon are high, which in February means cold nights. And the poverty in many of the villages creates feelings of sympathy for the people who must endure such hardship. But, all in all, a Mexican caravan is a great learning experience and a heck of a lot of fun.

If you're interested in having a peak experience south of the border, several companies offer guided RV tours to Copper Canyon, including Adventure Caravans, (800) 872-7897; Fantasy RV Tours, (800) 952-8496; and Tracks to Adventure, (800) 351-6053.

■ ■ ■

February 2002

Almost Yuman

Amotorhome's primary purpose is to allow its owner to be in his own home—be it temporarily or permanently—wherever he wants, whenever he wants. That's its biggest difference from regular homes, whose owners are stuck with where they are regardless of the weather, the neighbors, and local attractions.

Margie and I have chosen to be reasonably warm year-round, so we are snowbirds. Every year when I hear the honks of the Canada geese overhead at our home in Idaho, something in my genes starts pulling my inner-compass pointer to the south. And an inner voice whispers, "Surely you are as smart as a goose." Feeling that I am at least as smart as a silly goose, I line up the motorhome with that compass pointer and head for the Sun Belt.

We prefer arid climate to humid, which limits us to the Southwest. Anyone who has visited southern Arizona knows that this is dry country, but it is also sunny country Although it is unbearably hot in the summer, winters are great. According to statistics published by the Yuma Chamber of Commerce and generally verified by my more than twenty years' experience, the average maximum daily temperature in February is 73.5°F and the minimum average is 39.6°F. The wind kicks up the dust a few times each winter, but most of the time the air is clean and clear.

As with all cities, large or small, Yuma has its share of crime. However, it isn't the kind that affects the daily living of RV snowbirds. As for the pace of living, that's entirely up to the individual. A few people I know seem to be rushed a bit at times—making an early tee time, getting to a restaurant before the early-bird rates end, or getting to the swap meet early enough to get a close-in parking place. Most snowbirds, though, are more inclined to throttle back and assume a more relaxed attitude.

Yuma is a haven for those who like to eat out, and most RVers are in that category. Although most of the restaurants won't make the great dining lists, they are plentiful and modestly priced. Due to Yuma's proximity to Mexico and its large Hispanic population, there are lots of Mexican restaurants. Great controversies arise over which one is best.

Yuma's RV parks come in all sizes, types, and prices, ranging from those with only basic services to fine resorts. Most parks are in a mid-range in both amenities and prices, offering nice clubhouses, pools, horseshoe pits, pool tables, and card rooms. Some have ballrooms and offer weekly dances. Besides the normal amenities, some of the larger resorts have small golf courses, shuffleboard courts, whirlpool spas, and craft rooms, as well as full-time recreation directors who organize activities for park guests. Monthly rates vary from just under $300 to over $400 ($10–$13 per day). Seasonal or annual rates considerably reduce per-day costs for 'birds who wish to spend five months or more at the same park.

When the Spaniards arrived in the sixteenth century, they found Native Americans at what later became a well-used ferry crossing at the confluence of the Colorado and Gila rivers. Called Yumans until the 1950s, the Native Americans (now called by their tribal names, Quechans and Cocopahs) figure prominently in Yuma's commercial life. Their casinos draw thousands of visitors.

What is now the city of Yuma became a part of the United States with the Gadsden Purchase in 1854. Since then, it has figured prominently in the history of the Southwest. The old Territorial Prison, which was made famous by book authors and Hollywood, still stands (in ruins) as an Arizona state park. I have visited its museum many times, and I'm sure I'll do so again. Other historical mementos of Yuma's past that are open to the public include the Yuma Crossing Historical Park and the Century House Museum.

For some folks, Yuma represents Hicksville. They want the bright lights of the city with all the cultural trappings. But I love the ambiance, particularly of Historic Downtown Yuma, which has undergone a resurrection. Main Street now teems with pedestrians, sometimes enjoying festivals, arts-and-crafts shows, or musical events.

Only a twemty-minute drive from Yuma is Algodones, Mexico, where many snowbirds shop for medicines, curios, and gifts for the folks back home. Also, many people take advantage of the greatly reduced prices for dentistry and optometry there.

Yuma is growing. Last summer, it was listed by *Time* magazine as one of the top fifteen fastest-growing metropolitan areas in the United States. Apparently some people besides me think it's a great place. In fact, I like it so well and have spent so much time there that I'm almost Yuman.

■ ■ ■

March 2002

Modern Conveniences?

I t is with ambivalent feelings that I take keyboard in hand to write this column. I love the convenience that word processing provides, especially the Delete key. It s so easy to correct the mistakes I am prone to make. And the spellchecker is a lifesaver. I would hate to be without this wonderful invention, but it frustrates and infuriates me at times because I don't understand it.

The same goes for many of the other gadgets and machines that we take for granted today: cell phones, e-mail, telephone-answering machines that can be activated from other phones, mind-boggling music machines—everything electronic and computerized. I especially appreciate the wireless headphones that I use to overcome my hearing problem when I'm watching television. Yep, these marvelous inventions of the final quarter of the 1990s have changed our lives, generally for the better, but not in every way, every day.

On our way from Idaho to Yuma, Arizona, where we spend most of the winter, I hit a piece of steel in the road and blew an inside dual tire on the motorhome. No problem, you say? Just call emergency road service on my wonderful cell phone. I tried, but guess what? No phone service in the desert between Vidal Junction, California, and Parker, Arizona. After unhooking the car and driving about ten miles, I managed to get through to Camping World's Roadcare and got the problem taken care of. And that was just the beginning of my electronic-problems week.

Arriving at our destination with some service questions requiring answers, I needed to communicate with (a) the power company, (b) the phone company, and (c) the cable-TV company. Since none of those companies employ humans, I played the "press this, press that" game for three days with their electronic systems. Regrettably, I'm not too swift about their games, so they won most of the time. Too often, I couldn't figure out a button for a category that pertained to my questions, so I just wanted to throw in the towel. But, with Margie's prodding, I persisted and eventually got all my problems solved. Of course, that was after what seemed like hours of listening to that same voice telling me over and over that all of their customer service representatives were busy and to wait for the next one available. I am having nightmares in which I am instructed by a disembodied voice to "press 1 for this, press 2 for that, or 3 for something else" and I don't know what to press. (Margie denies being that disembodied voice.)

I have really been driven crazy trying to figure out the instructions for using some of my new equipment. My new computer had already been set up by my very computer-literate granddaughter, Heidi, but she just assumed that I could figure out the new printer, which remained in the box until we got to Yuma. How did I know a printer didn't come with a cable to hook it up to a computer? And how was I to know that there are different kinds of cables? Well, in only two days plus a call to Heidi, I had the printer working.

Then there was the new-TV problem. Since I hadn't bought a new set for quite a few years, I wasn't aware of some of the complications of setting one up on a cable system. Add the fact that I don't read instruction booklets unless I have to; I just plug in a thing and turn it on and expect it to work. With the new Sony and the accompanying remote control, I had to change my modus operandi totally; I read and reread, punched this and punched that over and over, and in only two days I got it all to work. I want to see some movies, but I'm afraid to tackle the necessary add-on.

The new cordless telephone with the built-in answering machine was actually pretty simple. Of course, I quit messing with it as soon as I got a dial tone.

Another modern way of doing things that frustrates me is how things are packaged in such a way that they're apparently never intended to be opened, at least by normal humans. Everything is prepackaged in not child-proof, but human-proof, plastic. Those hard plastic covers that make it convenient for stores to display small items are impossible to tear apart. We've learned to get knives or scissors every time we bring home those infernal packages.

I know the answer to these problems is simply to avoid them entirely. As the idealists in this lifestyle point out, all you have to do is go somewhere out in the boonies where you don't have to operate electronic gadgets or open newly purchased items. Just park under some tall trees by a rushing stream, plug into the sunshine and fresh air, and let the rest of the world go by

Good idea. By the time this column comes out, I'll be parked in the boondocks at Quartzsite. Hope I can make it till then.

■ ■ ■

April 2002

Caveat Emptor!

I n his *History of Roman Commerce,* the famous Roman historian Magna Bunkus reports that Roman-chariot salesman Edvardus Quickus (known in modern times as Fast Eddie) frequently told customers that his chariots would perform in ways that proved later to be untrue. Julius Simplus, the victim of a recent fall from a turnip chariot, purchased a used one. Knowing that he would encounter some steep hills in his travels selling "second-time-around" togas to country folks, Julius asked if the chariot would climb all the steep grades on the Appian Way with only two horses. Edvardus emphatically declared two horses would easily take that special chariot right over the Alps. Julius believed him and shelled out his life savings for the vehicle.

Much to his dismay, after he had purchased the chariot, Julius found that he barely made it over six of the Seven Hills of Rome, let alone the steepest grades on the Appian Way with his two-horsepower rig. He needed four horses. Complaining to the owner of Pompey's Used Chariots that he was sold something that would not perform as promised, Julius discovered a great truth that has plagued buyers for centuries: A salesman's verbal promises are meaningless to many business owners, who depend on their salespeople for profits. Nor did it cut any ice with the Senate when Julius took the matter to court. There he learned that the only thing that counts legally when push comes to shove is what is in writing.

The same day that Julius bought his used chariot, he got to daydreaming about all the wonderful places he could visit during his vacations. A very special resort-city came to mind—Pompeii—a popular hangout for rich and famous Romans. So Julius visited the sales office of an elegant resort that sold timeshares to folks who couldn't afford to buy their own places. With magnificent Mount Vesuvius in the background, it was a highly prized place for summer vacations and for communal bathing.

So Julius bought a timeshare that was good for two weeks in August. The salesman, Flavius Flakus (now known as Freddie the Flake), a jovial fellow, painted a verbal picture that soon had Julius salivating. He even promised that Julius could have free use of the stable for his horses and a place to park his chariot while he was enjoying his condo and the public baths.

Again, Julius relied on the word of the salesman, but, much to his chagrin, when he arrived at Pompeii on the allotted date, he found that it would cost him two months' wages to use the "free" stables and parking lot. And when he complained to the timeshare company's management about the salesman's promise, he had the same results as with his chariot deal.

The saga of Julius Simplus ends with his not only having to buy two more horses to pull the steep grades on the Appian Way, but unable to use his timeshare because he couldn't afford the parking fee. (But, in a way, he lucked out because he wasn't there when Vesuvius blew up and buried all those debauched people in Pompeii.)

Buyers often equate what they want to be true with what a salesperson says is true. In fact, some salesmen exhort trainees to tell the customer what he wants to hear. Some businesses, particularly used-auto dealerships, have become famous for dealing carelessly with the facts.

Unfortunately, there have been cases of RV dealers employing the same sales tactics used by the stereotypical used-car salesman, which has created some apprehension and distrust of RV dealers generally. It's unfortunate that the actions of a few tarnish the images of the many.

Two segments of the campground industry that have suffered some Fast Eddie image problems are those that sell memberships and those that sell lots. A few decades ago, this unregulated industry was open to all kinds of predatory practices with very little opportunity for legal redress. Nowadays, laws prohibit most of the evils of the past. Most folks who own campground memberships or their own lots find it a great way to go.

To avoid potential pitfalls with any major purchase, a buyer should carefully research the product first. Often a remorseful buyer's problem was created by himself; he simply didn't take the time and make the effort to know and understand what he should have known up front. And a buyer should always get it in writing. A salesperson eager for a commission may find the temptation to make promises that can't be kept irresistible.

Julius Simplus should have read the brochure more carefully and test-driven that chariot before he bought it. He should have read the small print on that timeshare contract. As he and millions of buyers after him have belatedly discovered, caveat emptor was wise advice 2,000 years ago and it still is today.

■ ■ ■

May 2002

The Checkout

A favorite and oft-played game of brand-new motorhome owners is "I wonder." After they have taken delivery and are using their new rigs for the first time, they wonder how you do this, how you do that, what this gizmo is for, or where the control or switch is for something.

It's unbelievable how many people spend weeks, months, or even years shopping for a motorhome and then leave the dealership after a twenty-minute explanation of how their new, very complicated machine works. On their first outings, they discover that all that glitz and glamour they focused on in the showroom loses much of its charm when they have full holding tanks and don't know how to empty them.

New buyers aren't the only players in the "I wonder" game. Even the veteran RVer who buys one of today's marvelous rigs—especially a diesel pusher—sometimes finds himself in a quandary about how some of the controls and gadgets work.

The problem is mainly due to the failure of RV dealers to provide good education at the time a new owner takes delivery of his coach. In some dealerships, that checkout responsibility is given to the salesperson who sold the motorhome; in others, it is a duty of the service department. In many cases, the checkout person is not qualified to do this very important job and, as a consequence, the new buyer gets in trouble the first time he tries to use his new motorhome.

Not all the blame should be heaped on the dealer. Customers are also guilty of not being good students during the checkout procedure. For a first-time owner, the situation can be overwhelming, especially if the teacher is not good at his job. Having a great deal of knowledge about something is one thing; having the ability to pass that knowledge on to others is quite another. Too often, what should be a learning process for the new owner fails because either the teacher or the student (or both) is not doing the job very well.

Ideally, the customer checkout would begin with a motorhome that is in absolutely perfect condition. Each system would have been checked out thoroughly, everything that operates would be in operation or ready to operate. The checkout person at the dealership would be skilled both in the mechanical features of the motorhome and as a teacher. And, last but not least, the customer would be attentive and focused on what he or she is being shown.

Unfortunately, the amount of information that must be transmitted in this checkout procedure is, for many people, too much for one lesson. For a first-time buyer, it can be absolutely overwhelming. The person giving the checkout instruction needs to be able to determine if his student is understanding the lesson, and the student shouldn't hesitate to ask questions or ask for a repeat of a demonstration if he doesn't get it the first time. If you are embarrassed to show ignorance now, I can assure you that it will be a lot more embarrassing to show that ignorance in a campground when you have to ask your neighbor or the campground owner how to operate your fine new motorhome.

Most of the instruction can best be done by demonstration. For example, the water-fill and holding-tank draining procedures "show" better than they "tell." In fact, a new owner should not only see how every operation is done, but he should do it himself at least once to make sure that he understands how things work.

Some dealers have hookups on the premises or have arrangements with nearby campgrounds for their customers to make their shakedown trips under supervision. That's the ideal way to start out. Any problems or misunderstandings can be caught and corrected with minor inconvenience. A new buyer who turns down such an invitation is missing a great opportunity to avoid more serious problems later.

An enormous change for many experienced motorhome owners in the past decade has been from gas engines to diesel. Many of us who have made that change have learned that it is a very different ball game in many respects. Driving and maintaining a diesel rig differ a great deal from driving and maintaining one with a gas engine. For those who are not particularly mechanically oriented, a thorough briefing by someone at the dealership (preferably a diesel technician) is a must. The alternative is to learn everything by experience—often the hard, sometimes expensive way.

Dealers owe it to their customers to offer the best information possible about the operation and maintenance of their new toys, taught by skilled teachers. And consumers owe it to themselves to learn those lessons before their first trip, so they won't have to play "I wonder" afterward.

■ ■ ■

June 2002

Front Porches

When I was a kid (a time referred to by my grandchildren as "the olden days"), most houses had front porches that served as a haven for relaxation and a vantage point for socializing. In the summer months, it was an important and much-used part of the home. Above all, it was a refuge from the hot interior of the house in those pre-air-conditioning days.

Porches come in various sizes, shapes, and appointments. I like those that were built in the early 1900s with a lot of gingerbread. Wicker chairs were often supplemented by a porch swing, which I particularly enjoyed. I can recall even now how my brothers and I used to get my grandma's swing up to top speed, both forward and sideways.

For adults, the front porch did double duty. Besides being a refuge from toil and turmoil, it was a greeting-and-meeting place. From their observation points on front porches, town folks could greet those who walked by on the sidewalks. Friends would stop by for conversation. Even people driving by were waved at in small towns where everyone knew everyone else. Front porches were perfect locations for gregarious people to interact with others.

Front porches were vantage points for Nosy Rosies to pursue their favorite pastime, too—seeing what was going on in town and converting it into gossip. They examined everyone who walked by, who was with whom, what they were wearing, who looked ill, who was pregnant, who appeared to be drinking.

And for young men and women, the porch swing was a great place for romance to flourish. Sitting in the dark and gently swinging, young couples could enjoy each other's company with no expense and little distraction.

I miss front porches. Often I drive through the old sections of towns, particularly small towns, just to look at old houses with front porches. Generally, they are on the main street and begin where the commercial area ends. Nearly all midwestern towns have old sections with big old houses that once were owned by the towns' wealthy people. In recent years, many have been purchased and remodeled by younger people who are interested in preserving and enjoying homes built for their grandparents' or great-grandparents' generations. Obviously, they are people who like front porches because most of those old houses have them.

Although the front porch is common in the Midwest, it is a feature of nearly all old houses in the South. Some were owned by famous people. I particularly like Henry Ford's house (across the street from Thomas Edison's) in Fort Myers, Florida. It has a huge porch on all sides and, like many houses in mosquito-infested areas, it is screened.

Not all houses with front porches were built for wealthy people. In fact, porches were a standard feature of the bungalows built in the 1920s and 1930s. Nearly all towns have sections where that type of house is still popular. Many have been remodeled with modern plumbing and electrical systems. Their popularity is due partly to the fact that they are affordable by people with modest incomes. Although among the less-expensive houses, many are well kept and comfortable. Most have porch swings and wicker chairs, and, on warm evenings, some have occupants who wave and speak to passersby on the sidewalks.

Although front porches are enjoying a comeback, they are mostly for ornamentation. The backyard and television have won the popularity battle. Memories of the olden days, when a simpler life prevailed, will fade with my generation. Future historians might record the demise of the front porch as a cultural step backward.

However, all is not lost. It should be obvious to motorhomers that our extended awnings are a kind of front porch where the simple pleasures that porch sitters used to enjoy are again in vogue. In fact, we have combined the backyard with the front porch by putting our barbecue equipment out with televisions and other assorted comfort equipment. From that vantage point in any campground, any place, we can exchange pleasantries with passersby and keep informed about our neighbors' activities.

A campground or an RV park is like a small town. Occupants are close to their neighbors, and friendliness is the rule. In snowbird parks, where residents typically stay for several months at a time, those awning porches can get pretty elaborate. Guests are entertained outdoors. Unlike the old-fashioned porch of yesteryear where iced tea and cookies were popular, a common campground scene has a smoking barbecue and the clink of glasses.

Yes, Virginia, the front porch, although changed, is alive and well.

■ ■ ■

August 2002

The Innocent Camper

You might recall Julius Simplus as the untutored chariot buyer who was thoroughly fleeced by the chariot salesman Edvardus Quickus (Fast Eddie), and again by Flavius Flakus (Freddie the Flake), with a much-misrepresented time-share membership. Having discovered the impracticality of using the time-share membership in Pompeii due to the unreasonably high cost of parking his horses and chariot, Julius made another one of his ill-thought-out decisions. Although he knew nothing about the lifestyle, he decided to take up chariot camping.

Knowing that he would need shelter from the elements, he made a chariot-tent, precursor of the station-wagon tent of the 1950s. With only his chariot-tent, a sack of oats for his horses, a few hastily packed personal possessions, and his faithful dog, Canis Sleepus, Julius headed north. No map, no supplies, and, the greatest mistake of all, no campground directory.

Since Julius didn't know where he was going, he had no way of knowing when he got there. Consequently, he drove until well after the sun had gone down. Finally, he spied campfires along the road and figured it was a place to camp. Pulling into the campground long past bedtime, with a clattering of hoofs, creaking of wheels, and much shouting at his horses, he found a vacant spot to pitch his chariot-tent. Interpreting the curses hurled by the sleep-disturbed occupants of other tents as cries of welcome, he finally settled in for the night.

Being an early riser, Julius was up before dawn to make preparations for another day on the road. With no regard for the noise he was making, he warmed up his horses for another day with a breakfast of oats.

While they were munching noisily away, Julius busied himself with taking down his chariot-tent and stowing his gear. After what seemed like an eternity to his fellow campers, he rumbled out of the campground in a cloud of dust, as their curses bade him farewell.

Because his route was completely unplanned, Julius unknowingly followed one of the steepest roads over the Alps. With his low-horsepower problem, he found himself moving very slowly and chariots with more horsepower backing up behind him. Unaware of road courtesy that requires slow-moving vehicles to pull over as soon as possible to allow faster vehicles to pass, he ignored all pull-out opportunities. Soon many chariots formed a great line behind him. Drivers fretted and fumed, and some screamed epithets and threats. A furious few hurled spears at Julius, and when one whizzed by his left ear, close enough for him to hear the "swish," he realized that something was amiss and pulled over to the side of the road.

After successfully crossing the Alps and remembering the difficulty he had in setting up camp after dark the previous night, Julius decided to find a campsite while there was still daylight. Luckily, as he rounded a curve, looming before him was a city. As he approached it, he spied a Super Gaul-Mart with a huge parking lot. In one corner near the road, many chariots were parked. Their owners had campfires burning, around which men were sitting on rocks and drinking wine while their women flipped pizza dough.

Julius pulled in to join the group, but several of the men recognized him as the noisy neighbor at the previous campground and the road hazard on the way up the mountains. Their threatening looks and gestures with swords gave Julius reason to set up camp on the other side of the parking lot, where he settled in for the night. In fact, he liked the place so well, especially the free-parking aspect, that he settled in for an indefinite stay. Only with the encouragement of the Gaul-Mart manager did he finally hit the road.

Some of Julius' descendants are still out there in motorhomes. We've all encountered them. They come in the campground just as you're trying to go to sleep, or they leave an hour before sunrise, after warming their engine for twenty minutes. Their dogs run free. They refuse to pull out for faster traffic on mountain roads, and they set up their camps at Wal-Mart with awnings extended, chairs out, and a char-broiler smoking.

We can all learn from Julius's experiences. First, we should have some knowledge of the lifestyle we are embarking on, the proper equipment, and how to use it. We should know where we are going when we hit the road and plan for early stops and quiet starts that don't disrupt the lives of our fellow campers. If we have pets, we should walk them in the prescribed places and control them at all time. We should be considerate of other drivers when on the road. And finally, when we enjoy the hospitality of businesses that permit overnight use of their parking lots, we should be overnighters, and that's all.

As motorhomers, we are very visible. Let's present a good picture.

■ ■ ■

September 2002

Those Extra Pounds

At a party a few weeks ago in the RV park where we stay during the winter, there were fourteen men present. Thirteen of us had "Dunlap's disease"; we "done lap over" at the midsection. None of us is grossly fat, but all except one are packing pounds that any half-way intelligent person should know are impairing our health and probably shortening our lives.

The obvious questions are: How and why did we get this way? Do we really not care about how long and how well we live? Are we not bothered by the fact that our clothes are often tight and that it takes very little physical exertion to poop us out? Have we lost interest in how we appear to others? And, finally, is there a solution to the problem?

Some of the answers are simple. We got this way because we eat too much of the wrong foods and we exercise too little. One of the blessings of retirement is that we don't have to work, so we don't have to get up early in the morning and get going. And we don't have to do anything all day if we don't want to. It's also a curse.

Although most of us don't suddenly turn into inert lumps of clay, few of us expend as many calories as we did during our working days. Of course, that is in addition to the almost automatic slowdown that occurs as we work through and past middle age. The consequence is that a surplus of fat calories is accumulated that, with men, go right to the midsection. A sure sign of this unwelcome change in a man's physique is the necessity to get new pants a size larger. It is a progression for many of us through the thirties and into the forties. I can recall the steps upward from a size 32. When I reached size 38 a few years ago,

Margie threatened me with divorce if I ever hit 40. Fortunately, she backed down from that position.

Dunlaps's disease is an insidious malady. It creeps up ounce by ounce, oh so slowly. Symptoms are there, like the need to let out another notch on a belt. But as long as there's another notch to go to, we don't really pay much attention to the change. Actually we don't see it at all until we discover that we need another notch and there isn't one there. Now it takes a longer belt, which should be an alarm that we aren't doing something right. However, most of us just ignore that alarm and we go our merry way.

As for caring how well and how long we live—well, I'm sure all of us would like to have good health, be comfortable in performing whatever tasks we have, and live a long time (whatever that is). We're all aware of our physical condition when we get up and down or have to exert ourselves with some manual task that we used to perform regularly with ease, but now huff and puff doing it. We recognize the problem at the moment, but I guess most of us don't concern ourselves about what is happening to our bodies enough to care for them properly.

Ironically, many of us take better care of our motorhomes than we do of ourselves. Few of us neglect regular maintenance—oil changes, lube jobs, tire pressure, fluid levels, etc., but we fail to take the same care of our own bodies.

As for looks, I'm sure that many of us have lost that great need to be admired for our physical appearances. There's not enough peer pressure among older, overweight people to eat and exercise properly. We're all in the same boat. And, unfortunately, we aren't as concerned about conveying the masculine look that obsessed many of us in our mating years.

So, what can we do about it? Unfortunately, that awful four-letter word *diet* and its companion, *exercise*, are the only answers. Very simply, the eating habits that we have developed over many decades have to be changed. And the exercise or lack-of-exercise habits that we have fallen into have to be given up. The only answer is to eat right and exercise right. The irony is that everyone could change the situation for the better, but few do.

Many of us try to do something positive about our condition and usually fail. Habit can be a terrible thing. It's hard to break bad ones and develop new good ones. I know; I'm trying again. Without being radical about changing the way I live, at Margie's insistence and with her assistance, I'm changing the way I eat to include more of the things that I know I should eat (asparagus, carrots, broccoli, apples, bananas) and I'm leaving out many of the things I love (quarter-pounders, French fries, potatoes, cake, pie). And I walk a lot. Fortunately, my little dog, Suzie, loves to go on walks, morning, noon and night.

Between Margie and Suzie, and with a new attitude on my part, perhaps I can again use some of those size 38 pants that I've been saving for four years. Heck, I'm sure Margie wouldn't mind buying some new size 36s for me.

■ ■ ■

October 2002

Home, Sweet Home

After a leisurely seven-month sojourn in southern climes, we arrived home in Idaho's Panhandle near the end of May to witness for ourselves the ravages of an unusually severe winter. Heavy snowpacks had melted and refrozen many times with additional snows and rains in between. Eventually the watery snow "turned to concrete," as my neighbor put it. A tool shed that had been standing for more than twenty years had a caved-in roof; a cedar-rail fence along the driveway was broken; large limbs from maple trees in the yard had broken off; and deck railing around the house had pulled loose. So the first week at home was spent making repairs.

The good news was that the heavy snows and rain had provided much-needed moisture to the soil that was parched from the previous dry summer. Everything that grows had grown twice as fast as normal with the advent of spring, which of course included our two-acre lawn, now a foot high. Fortunately the lawn mower started right up, and in a mere five hours the yard had a lived-on appearance. To keep that great green look, I spent another couple hours giving it a good dose of fertilizer. That means it will grow three times as fast, which will require more five-hour mowing jobs.

Then there's our big garden. Of course, the first crop of the spring is always a variety of weeds, some of which have roots that reach halfway to China. Rototilling follows, and as I struggle to keep the tiller going straight, I think of those TV commercials showing a lady holding one handle as the machine churns the soil. What a difference between advertising and reality!

After two weeks of hard labor in the garden, everything is planted (they almost had to plant *us*). Now we can pull and hoe weeds, spray bugs, water, and tend all the good veggies as they grow during the next three months.

Naturally, everything ripens or matures at one time, so what do two people do with all that produce? The answer is simple: Give it away to the kids, friends, and neighbors, and almost anyone who happens to drop by. I have a rule in the summer, though. If you take peas or beans or lettuce or other good stuff, you also have to take zucchini. Some friends lock their cars when visiting, so I can't fill them up with veggies when they aren't looking. We leave home in October with jars and boxes of stuff to distribute wherever we go. Potatoes, carrots, beets, tomatoes, and apples fill the compartments of the motorhome. We call our produce "Idaho Care Packages." I don't know whether people appreciate our gifts, but they take them anyway.

We are pretty well caught up now, but our relaxation period will be brief. The little veggies will soon start to poke through the ground. Of course, the weeds will precede them and my trusty hoe will see plenty of action. And the knees-to-the-ground work of thinning carrots, beets, and lettuce will be a joint-challenging task. If the summer is another dry one, moving and adjusting sprinklers will be a regular chore.

Our large deck took a beating from the icy snow, so it will have to be stained. And just in case it gets cold before we leave in the fall, I'll cut, haul, and stack a cord or two of firewood for the fireplace. Besides the big jobs, there will be the maintenance on the mower, rototiller, and chain saw, as well as fence-mending, sprinkler-repairing, and painting. It takes sweat and money to maintain a country home in the north— especially if it sits empty six months a year.

Why does anyone do it? Particularly, why would an avid motorhomer put up with all this work (and expense) to own a high-maintenance home when he could live in a low-maintenance motorhome and loaf most of the time?

I guess the best answer is that we like to eat our cake and have it too. Like many motorhomers, we've been at it for thirty years (thirteen RVs and approximately a half-million miles), and we've loved it. But we've treasured the time spent at our special country retreat. During the summer months, our kids, grandkids, relatives, and friends visit our regular home. It's our opportunity to connect with family amidst the things that make a house a home.

As for the physical work, it's good for us. We use muscles that have been in hibernation all winter and toughen up a bit. Add the pleasure of walking in the garden early in the morning and the simple joy of seeing bean plants poking their little grasshopper heads through the soil. It's exciting to see things you've labored over turn into delicious fresh vegetables.

So, like many extended-time motorhomers who love to travel, but also love to have roots, we'll keep on motorhoming and keep returning to our "real home" every summer. You really can go home again—but have your work clothes ready.

■ ■ ■

November 2002

Emergency Preparations

argie and I find cemeteries interesting. In numerous places we've visited over the years, we've wandered through fields of tombstones, reading names, dates, epitaphs, and the miscellaneous information displayed on the blocks of granite that mark final resting places.

We particularly enjoy graveyards that have famous —or infamous— people buried in them. Some of my favorites are Boston, where Paul Revere and others associated with our Colonial period are conspicuous; or Charleston, South Carolina, where John C. Calhoun's tombstone is as large as his personality in history; or, quite the opposite, the rather inconspicuous grave of Kit Carson in Taos, New Mexico. I'm not sure about the authenticity of some of the markers on Boot Hill in Tombstone, Arizona; they seem a bit hokey. However, the barely marked graves at the old Territorial Prison at Yuma are, I am assured by state park rangers, very real, though they hold no one famous.

We have been amused by poetic, sometimes humorous, epitaphs, especially in gold rush towns in California. We are always saddened by the spectacle of hundreds of graves in military cemeteries at famous battlefields of the Civil War. Of course, the most famous of those is Arlington National Cemetery, where the Eternal Flame burns over President John F. Kennedy's grave.

The most important cemetery to us is a small one in southern Illinois. Situated off a county road, surrounded by woods, with several enormous cedars among the headstones, it holds many of my family members. Included are my great-great-great-grandfather, my great-great-grandfather, my great-grandfather and great-grandmother, my father and my mother, a sister, and other relatives. When visiting living relatives in the area, I always go to that cemetery and read the headstones again. We'll be there in a couple of months, and, for the first time, we'll see a headstone with our names on it.

There are no immediate plans to use our headstone, but it's inevitable that it will be used eventually. We actually are doing what every extended-time RVer should consider in planning for the future: preparing for our final trip. The fact that we are often away from home base creates a situation that can involve hardship in time and expense for the surviving spouse and other responsible kin. However, it is a situation that can be addressed sensibly before it becomes a fact.

Several years ago, we were in a snowbird park in Arizona when a lady passed away. Her husband was unwell and almost totally unable to cope with the situation. Newcomers to the park, they had no acquaintances who were knowledgeable about their family. As might be expected in an RV community, new neighbors came to the assistance of the distraught husband. Far-away children were called, but it was almost two days before any got there to make all the decisions that accompany the death of a family member.

Besides having to cope with the loss, the family was facing all the problems associated with death a long way from their homes. After hurried flights, lost sleep, providing details to local authorities, and making long-distance funeral arrangements, there was the added problem of what to do about the motorhome. It was a nightmare for the husband and children because they were facing problems for which no preparations had been made, including extraordinary expenses. That is a scenario that doesn't have to happen.

Extended- or full-time RVers live unusual lives. Adjustments have to be made to cope with the realities the lifestyle presents. Included in the preparations are some "in case of an emergency" plans. Sensible people make wills and provide for the disposition of their possessions and the handling of other matters before they pass away. There's one more thing we can do to make things easier and less expensive for our survivors: Arrange for our final emergency.

Besides making it easier emotionally for survivors, making arrangements in advance can save money. When decisions are made hastily during times of emotional stress, unscrupulous funeral-parlor operators may charge outlandish prices.

Margie and I have made plans that will alleviate some of the problems associated with our deaths. No matter where we are when that happens, one simple call to a toll-free number (we each carry a card with instructions) is all it will take to make things happen. A funeral parlor near the family cemetery will take care of everything from that point. It's all paid for.

We don't look at our plans as being morbid or negative. We're just being realistic, sensible, and thoughtful. All RVers should think about making preparations for this kind of emergency.

■ ■ ■

January 2003

Easy Payments

This month, we catch up again with Julius Simplus, the itchy-footed Roman who took up chariot camping at a Gaul-Mart parking lot in what is now France. With a used chariot and two horses, he had taken to the road with his dog, Canis Sleepus, to escape the fast pace of city life in Rome and sell used togas to country folks. Unfortunately, Julius's knowledge of the camping lifestyle was zilch. In his ignorance, Julius did about everything wrong.

To begin with, Julius relied on the word of Edvardus Fastus (Fast Eddie), a used-chariot salesman who sold him a rig totally unsuitable for its intended purpose, but which earned Edvardus a hefty commission. Then he was fast-talked by Flavius Flakus (Freddie the Flake) into a timeshare membership that proved to be entirely too expensive to maintain. And in his first few days on the road, he angered his fellow charioteers on mountain passes with his refusal to pull over and let faster traffic go around him, and his fellow campers with inconsiderate campground etiquette.

We find him now continuing that pattern of ignorance and insensitivity by spending his sixth day in the parking lot at the Gaul-Mart. With a campfire blazing most of the night, his horses doing their horse-things, and Canis Sleepus doing his dog-things all over the place, Julius was finally asked by the store manager to move on.

Following the road that led to what we now know as the English Channel, across which Caesar had led his army a few years before, Julius met many fellow campers during his nightly stops. At one place, he was intrigued by a band of gypsies and enthralled by their music, colorful garb, and, particularly, their vehicles. In fact, he was absolutely smitten by one owned by the leader, Wily Roma.

It was a wagon with a cute little house built on it—green, with two windows with yellow shutters, four wheels with silver spokes, and a chimney protruding from the roof, which meant cooking inside and having a warm place to sleep. And, the frosting on the cake—four white horses hitched up to it. Unbelievably, it had a FOR SALE sign on it. He had to have that rig.

What Julius didn't know was that the owner of the rig had been watching. Sensing a pigeon, he emerged from the door, poised for the kill.

When Julius inquired why the rig was being sold, Wily launched into a long story about how his wife was ill and her only chance to live rested with a famous doctor in Spain. He was sacrificing his beautiful rig to get the money for the operation that would save his wife's life. It all sounded reasonable to Julius who bit—hook, line, and sinker.

Wily invited Julius inside to take a look at all the bells and whistles. A shiny black iron stove stood at one end next to a cupboard filled with bowls and jugs of foods. A dining table and four bunk beds were hinged to the wall and could be folded up to allow more living space. A copper washbasin sat on an enclosed cabinet which, when opened, revealed a hidden chamber pot. But topping all those wonderful amenities was the water tank on the roof that provided sun-warmed water to both the kitchen and the bathroom!

Mrs. Roma had done a marvelous job of interior decorating. There were cute curtains at the windows, colorful vases filled with wildflowers, scented candles emitting heavenly aromas, bearskin rugs on the floor, even a mirror on the wall by the washbasin.

Going outside, Wily showed Julius the four beautiful horses that pulled the wagon. As with most men, Julius was mesmerized by the thought of doubling the horsepower he presently had. Wily lifted up a horse's hoof to show its perfect horseshoes, he pulled back the horse's lips to show its perfect teeth, and he assured Julius that the young horses were good for a lot of miles. And although they were big and powerful, the horses didn't require much food. In fact, claimed Wily, "They give 50 miles per feeding of oats." (Later Julius found that figure was about half the reality.)

Fearing that the price would be beyond his means, Julius asked, "How much?" His fears were justified. The price would take his life savings of gold dinarii—plus MCMXCIX (1999) dinarii more. Julius's hopes were fading fast when Wily came up with a magic solution: "Tell you what I'm gonna do," he said. "You can pay the balance in CCXD (240) easy payments."

Although his head was telling him, "No," Julius's heart was telling him, "Go for it."

His heart won, and that's why a destitute Julius lives in his gorgeous but permanently parked rig next to Wily Roma's stable. The foolish Roman spends his days shoveling manure to pay for his "trading-up" folly. And his dreams of life on the road have turned into a nightmare.

There must be a lesson or two here for twenty-first-century RV enthusiasts.

■ ■ ■

February 2003

Life on Wheels—Rollin'

"**P**eople who know more go more." That's the slogan of the RV consumer-education program that I helped develop at the University of Idaho eight years ago, which has been expanded to colleges in three other states. One purpose of this unique program is to help people who would like to be RVers, but have uncertainties about what the lifestyle is all about and whether or not they are suited for it. Often they are in a quandary about what type, size, brand, and floorplan to choose, and rightfully so. After all, they are probably going to be spending the largest sum of money they have ever spent at one time on something that they aren't sure whether or not they will like. Education can provide much of the answer.

Many RV buyers make their purchase completely blind the first time. That's not the best way to do it. However, I've talked to people who went from zero knowledge to ownership of a $200,000 motorhome directly to fulltiming with only a dream and lived happily ever after. They were the lucky ones.

Getting the necessary knowledge to understand the RV lifestyle and the machines used in that way of life isn't easy. More often than not, people learn from experience. That's the hard way. Of course, you can always get ideas from RVing friends.

Some RV shows offer seminars for the public. For years, Margie and I traveled a circuit, doing three seminars a day at shows ranging from Florida to Pennsylvania to California. We left that circuit eight years ago to retire, but retirement wasn't in the cards.

After some thirty years of RVing at the time of our "retirement" and more than twenty years of writing for TL Enterprises publications, I was aware of the need for more formal RV education both for wannabes and experienced RVers. Since we live at a time when there are educational opportunities for all ages on all kinds of subject matter, I saw an opportunity to open doors.

And that's how the Life on Wheels conference came about at the University of Idaho. Its success led to the development of similar programs at Bowling Green, Kentucky; Harrisburg, Pennsylvania; and Des Moines, Iowa.

Life on Wheels conferences are not geared to any particular experience level. Some classes are aimed at the wannabe; many others are geared to the needs of the fulltimer. Approximately 20 percent of the attendees at each conference do not yet own RVs. They've come to learn all they can before they plunk down money for that new rig. The other 80 percent represent various levels of experience; many of them are fulltimers.

Generally about one-third of the classes are technical in nature—how to maintain the various RV systems, electronic devices that fit the RV lifestyle, solar power, etc. Another third concern the daily living aspect of RV life—choosing an RV, where to go, what to do, several views of fulltiming, etc. The other third deals with lifestyle enhancement topics, such as photography, cooking, health maintenance, security, etc. In short, there's something for everyone.

I'm proud of the core instructional staff we've rounded up for Life on Wheels. Joe and Vicki Kieva write columns for *Highways* and Woodall's, do a huge seminar circuit and write books; Bill Farlow (a fulltimer for sixteen years) is technical editor for *Coast to Coast* and has authored three books; Sharlene "Charlie" Minshall (a solo fulltimer for fifteen years) has written five books about her adventures; Dave and Sandy Baleria (both former law-enforcement officers) are personal-safety experts; Steve Savage (a master certified technician) is an expert on just about every mechanical or electrical system in an RV; Mac

McCoy (a former fire-safety trainer) teaches classes in how to prevent and fight RV fires; Greg Holder is recognized as the leading expert in solar power for RVs; and Mike Steffen covers many bases, both technical and lifestyle enhancement.

The point is that there's little reason for a wannabe to jump into the RV lifestyle cold turkey or for the old pro not to get a new perspective. Although it takes some time, travel, and money,

RV education is available at Life on Wheels conferences. The nearly 6,000 students who have attended one or more of the programs have been unanimous in their praise of our efforts to help RVers know more so they will go more—and, by inference, to more fully enjoy a lifestyle that is hard to beat.

For more information about upcoming Life on Wheels conferences, see lifeonwheels.com or call (866) LOW-GOGO (569-4646).

■ ■ ■

March 2003

Motorhomes for Shallow Pockets

C hances are that regardless of one's age, buying an RV will be one of the largest—if not the largest—purchase one will ever make. That's especially true if that RV is a new motorhome. And therein lies a problem for families just starting out in the RV lifestyle.

Fortunately for younger buyers who haven't accumulated their "pile" yet, several manufacturers have introduced Class C models that carry lower price tags than we have seen in a long time. In the past year, I've noted several brands at RV shows that had retail price tags (show specials) as low as $36,995. Although I have memories of Class Cs in the late 1960s and early 1970s priced at $6,995, I have become so accustomed to the change in the value of money that $36,995 strikes me as an incredibly low price today.

Of course, those low-enders are not only low priced, but they are very small by today's standards. Most are around 20 to 21 feet long, which, when compared to the most popular Class As that are sold today (ranging from 34 to 40 feet), are indeed tiny. However, they are big enough for most families. I know that from personal experience; our first two motorhomes were 19 and 21 feet respectively, and we did just fine.

In those days, we, as most young families, were much more inclined to go camping; that is, most of our nights were spent in public campgrounds and our activities were outdoors. We had campfires and did most of our eating at campground picnic tables. And we didn't have

TV. Entertainment had to be found at the beach, in the woods, or out in the desert. Usually that meant that the kids met other kids and they found things to do together. As for me, I could be perfectly content in the evening beside a campfire with a lantern on a pole behind my camp chair, a book in hand, and, possibly, a snifter of brandy (snake-bite prevention, which really works because I've never been bitten by a snake while camping).

I've even seen some Class As with price tags under $50,000. As with low-priced Class Cs, they were quite short (22 feet), but at that price one shouldn't expect more. Our first Class A was a 21-foot Shasta, and we loved it. In fact, we attended our first Good Sam national rally in it at Lincoln, Illinois, in 1975. With a Chevy 350 engine, we got great mileage, and, due to its light weight, we navigated some roads that I wouldn't dare venture on today with my much larger and heavier rig. Then we followed some of the gray roads through some great back-country and good fishing. Again, that's something we wouldn't dare to tackle today.

My point is that small isn't necessarily bad. In fact, small motorhomes can fill the bill nicely. If you are the adventurous type who likes the freedom to travel on almost any road that a car or a pickup can, then a 20- to 22-foot motorhome might be just the ticket for you.

New motorhomes are great, not only because they are brand-new, but also because they come with warranties on both the chassis and the coach and its components. So there's the security of knowing for a period of time that if something breaks it will be taken care of at no cost to you.

For those who cannot or don't want to put out the money for a new rig—not even a very low priced one—this is a great time for used-motorhome buyers. With the almost universal popularity of slide-outs, motorhomes without them are in the same category as three-bedroom houses with one bath. The result is that many dealers' lots are loaded with non-slideout motorhomes that are very reasonably priced. Also, many private parties have their rigs for sale via classified ads in various publications (newspapers, TL publications, the Internet, *RV Search*, *RV Trader*, etc.) or parked in their driveways with For Sale signs on them.

Shopping private owners is time consuming and usually involves phone calls, appointments, and driving considerable distances to see the rigs. And one must always bear in mind that when you buy from a private owner, your guarantee usually expires at the end of the driveway. However, by being careful and taking time, the odds of making a good buy from a private party are quite good.

Attend RV shows, particularly large ones, for information on new rigs. The fact is that dealers are very competitive at these events, and that usually means that they put their best price forward. Incidentally, many dealers have a bulletin board at shows with pictures of used rigs that they have available.

What I'm suggesting is that the person who wants to get into a motorhome at as low a price as possible should explore all these opportunities. My point is that you can become a motorhome owner even if your bank account is humble.

■ ■ ■

April 2003

Buying Used

I received a letter from a friend yesterday, asking for advice on buying a used motorhome. Actually his inquiry was for the benefit of his son, who knows little about motorhomes and has shallow pockets.

Rather than address the question in a return letter to my friend, I've decided to answer it here so others who are in similar circumstances might pick up a useful tip or two. I wouldn't advise taking my words as gospel, but during more than forty years in the RV business and some half-million miles on the road, I have developed some opinions that might be useful.

As with new motorhomes, the used market contains an incredible variety of offerings. You can find two-year-old bus conversions for nearly a million dollars, or you can find thirty-year-old low-enders for $2,500—and there's everything in between. A used-motorhome buyer has to set a price limit on what he/she can pay and then shop in that range.

To get an overview of what is available, a prospective buyer should do some basic research about what is on the market and what prices are like. There are numerous sources for that information, beginning with RV Search (rvsearch.com) and this magazine's classified section. *RV Trader*, which is available at some newsstands, and classified sections in most newspapers also advertise motorhomes for sale.

There are two excellent price guides: *Kelley Blue Book* (kbb.com) and the *N.A.D.A Appraisal Guide* (nadaguides.com). Usually they are available at public libraries. Banks have them, too. By noting both wholesale and retail prices for various years, you can get some idea of what fits your pocketbook.

Some people claim that one should always buy from a private party because individuals sell cheaper and are more likely to give honest information, but don't believe it. True, there are sometimes great buys from wonderful private owners, but there are also some high prices and/or defective rigs offered by not-so-wonderful others. If you buy from a private party, you have no recourse if you end up with a lemon. However, if you are a reasonably good judge of people, you can avoid the pitfalls that can be encountered with dishonest folks.

Although many used motorhomes are advertised in periodicals, most aren't. The only advertising many get is a FOR SALE sign in the window when parked in someone's driveway, parking lot, or other place where passersby can see it. Obviously, it behooves a motorhome shopper to stop and check out those opportunities. Sometimes there will be a sheet with information about the vehicle—including the price—taped to a window. Usually a phone number is included, so it's relatively easy to get additional information.

Now is a good time to visit motorhome dealers' lots. Many have an oversupply of non-slideout older models that they are offering at good prices. Often it is possible to get a limited warranty for a brief period, which is an advantage over buying from a private party. Also, a dealer can usually offer financing regardless of the age of the unit.

To a certain extent, when you buy a used motorhome, you buy a pig in a poke. But there are many things to look for that will reduce the odds of getting unexpected problems. Following is a list of some things to look for.

- *Body exterior*: Look for dings, paint scrapes, pitted siding, rock chips on the front cap and windshield, faded paint, loose trim, and cracked and/or delaminated fiberglass. If it looks great, it probably is; if it looks well used, it probably is.

- *Mechanical*: The fewer miles, the better; oil should be clean and the engine should look cared for; transmission fluid should be pink in color and should not smell burned; minimal tire wear; no suspension sagging; good brakes and lights. Ask to see the maintenance log if one is available. Take a test drive to check power, transmission, brakes, and suspension. If you aren't mechanically inclined, ask a friend who is to do the checkout with you.
- *Interior*: Anyone should be able to tell if the living quarters of a motorhome have been abused or not. A rig can have low miles but high occupancy, resulting in a worn interior. The condition of the upholstery, paneling, cabinets, drawers, bathroom, drapes, and other obvious features tell a story. Make sure all appliances work and appear to be well maintained. If the interior looks well used or abused, it probably has been; if it looks clean and nice, it probably is.

My final word of advice: *Take your time*. There probably is a used motorhome out there that is just right for you, but you have to do your homework and legwork and be patient.

■ ■ ■

May 2003

Different Strokes for Different Folks

One of the wonderful aspects of motorhoming is that we have so many options when it comes to where we use our rigs as homes. Self-containment allows us to have the comforts and services that we are accustomed to in regular houses, but the fact that we have an engine and wheels gives us the freedom to choose where that home will be situated.

The choices we have regarding where to park our motorhomes are many and varied. Basically, there's something for everybody, ranging from the very simple and inexpensive to the very luxurious and costly. Amenities vary from those that nature provides—sunshine, clear air, and solitude—to very complex man-made entertainment facilities, like golf courses, swimming pools, entertainment centers, ballrooms, tennis courts, and every conceivable creature comfort.

It is possible for motorhomers of modest means—and those who may not be poor, but don't like to spend money on campgrounds—to get by without spending anything for overnight spots. Truck stops, malls, or other large parking lots (particularly Wal-Marts), rest areas, friends' or relatives' driveways, various free government campgrounds (city, county, state, federal)—the possibilities for free places to stop overnight are many. They usually aren't very choice, nor do I recommend them as a regular way to camp.

Another often-inexpensive category of RV parking places involves camping in the traditional sense: amid woods, trees, lakes, and rivers; hiking, fishing, and making campfires; seeing and being involved with nature. State and federal campgrounds range from very primitive to full-service facilities. Some are quite inexpensive. For example, U.S. Forest Service campground fees vary between $5 and $10 (half-price for Golden Age Passport holders). However, many states have absolutely beautiful campgrounds with full-service sites that are comparable in price to private campgrounds.

The great advantage of state-park campgrounds is that they are almost invariably located in the most beautiful or special places in those states. A disadvantage for some people is the fact that they are usually located far from civilization—McDonald's, malls, and supermarkets.

For those who prefer private parks that feature man-made forms of fun and games, there are many options. Often the amenities consist primarily of things that appeal to kids, such as swimming, miniature golf, and game rooms, and are moderately priced. Family campgrounds are popular in heavily trafficked tourist areas such as Myrtle Beach, South Carolina; Mount Rushmore, South Dakota; Gettysburg, Pennsylvania; Gatlinburg, Tennessee; and other interesting places.

A growing group of campers seldom use the wheels of their RVs. They rent spaces in campgrounds on an annual basis and leave their rigs there much of the time, visiting on weekends and vacations. Actually, those campgrounds become little villages, communities where families share their leisure times with campground neighbors. I've seen motorhomes in campgrounds that have been parked so long that weeds have grown up around them, definitely not the way to treat an expensive motorhome.

A phenomenon of recent decades has been the upsurge of adults-only RV parks. That movement parallels the growth of adult retirement communities. Generally an age limit (usually fifty to fifty-five) restricts tenancy, and children aren't allowed. The rationale is that a lot of retirees prefer a child-free environment. Amenities and activities are geared to the preferences of those older folks. Snowbird parks in the Sun Belt almost invariably impose an age limit.

The present development of ultra-deluxe motorhome resorts that include unbelievably plush amenities such as golf courses, fine restaurants, and ballrooms, is mind-boggling. Some with huge spaces even offer custom-built activity buildings and elaborate patios with built-in barbecues, refrigerators, and sinks with hot and cold water. Lot prices at some of them exceed $200,000. They are definitely for rich folks, many of whom have motorhomes that cost more than a million dollars.

In short, there are campground options that fit the needs of nearly everyone and every pocketbook. No one should feel that motorhoming is a lifestyle that is geared to the needs or whims of any particular segment of our population.

Fortunately, campground directories, such as Trailer Life's and Woodall's, give us the necessary information to choose the kind of accommodations that fit our individual needs. It just takes a little homework to plan trips that take you to campgrounds that fit your style.

■ ■ ■

June 2003

Where Do You Hang Your Hat?

Catch-22: A fulltimer who wants no home, no city, and no state can't have what he wants. You can say that you don't live in any particular place, but the reality is that you have to claim that you do.

Every state requires that you have a license on your vehicle and a license to drive it, and those licenses are issued only to residents. Which state you claim is up to you, but, in most states, you must have a physical address there—a number on a street or road. Only in a few instances will a post office box number suffice. In short, you have to claim residence somewhere in order to be legally on the road, but, in so doing, you must claim something that isn't true and, in effect, break a law—Catch-22.

The good news is that as long as you conform to the other laws in the state, you aren't likely to get into trouble, but you are legally obliged to pay whatever taxes the state imposes on residents.

A problem in the past (and probably still, in some places) was that some fulltimers claimed residence in one state to avoid paying one tax and residence elsewhere to avoid another. For example, a person would purchase a motorhome in a state with no sales tax and give an address in that state, but he also would claim residence in another state to avoid state income tax. States with high sales taxes have been aggressive in catching and punishing residents who have purchased and licensed motorhomes in no-sales-tax states, and penalties have been severe. It has become a risky business to use dual citizenship to save money.

For most fulltimers, choosing a state for a home base isn't a big problem. If you don't have a large income, you don't have to worry about state income taxes. If your coach isn't really expensive or heavy, you generally won't have to pay a huge sum each year for a vehicle license. And if you don't own real estate, you won't pay property taxes.

On the other hand, you could have a substantial income, own an expensive motorhome, and face a real challenge when choosing a home base. If you have substantial taxable income, then consider the no-income-tax states: Alaska, Florida, Nevada, New Hampshire, South Dakota, Texas, and Washington. But there are other considerations.

Alaska imposes no sales-tax liability when out-of-state vehicles are registered and has an inexpensive license fee. However, Alaska does require a physical address, and the law is specific about residency requirements and penalties for violations.

Although New Hampshire has neither income nor sales tax, license fees are based on vehicle weight, so a license for a big motorhome can be pricey. There's also a tax when registering a vehicle from out of state and an annual vehicle-safety inspection that requires the registered owner's presence during his or her birthday month.

Nevada has inexpensive license fees and no income tax, but a high sales tax and a privilege tax based on a vehicle's value, and some counties impose a supplemental privilege tax. When out-of-state vehicles are registered, a relatively high tax is imposed.

Washington has no income tax, but a high sales tax. Credit is given for sales tax already paid in another state, but any difference must be paid. License fees are inexpensive; e.g., $30 for motorhomes.

Florida has long been a choice for many fulltimers. Not only does it have no income tax, but it has an inexpensive annual license fee ($46.60 for motorhomes of 4,500 pounds or more). However, registering vehicles from out of state can cost 6 percent if no sales tax has been previously paid (credit is given for tax already paid), and there is a $100-per-vehicle registration fee.

Texas also is a popular home-base state for fulltimers, partly because the Escapees Club provides members a legal address in a state with no income tax. However, be aware of costs involved to register out-of-state rigs; there's a $225 safety inspection and a $90 new-resident fee. License fees are $42 annually for motorhomes.

South Dakota is a state that's growing in popularity with fulltimers, partly due to the fact that a post office box suffices. There is no income tax and a low sales tax (4 percent). Registering rigs from out of state costs 3 percent, but reciprocity is granted for tax paid in another state, and license fees are reasonable.

In the United States, we have the right to be residents of whatever state we choose. None is perfect, but there's a "best state" for every pocketbook. To compare all the state taxes and registration fees, see the 2003 edition of *Selecting an RV Home Base*; call (800) 766-1674, or log on to tldirectory.com to order a copy. And before you make a decision, verify the current information with the appropriate state agencies.

■ ■ ■

July 2003

On the Road Again with Julius

A few months ago, we left Julius Simplus, a Roman camping wannabe, doomed to shoveling manure in Wily Roma's stable for the next twenty years. Julius was the victim of a clever sales pitch and an easy-payment plan for a glamorous new rig that he could not resist and certainly couldn't afford. But buying a rig that he couldn't afford was only the latest of Julius's goofs. Taking up chariot camping with absolutely no knowledge of the lifestyle got him started on the wrong foot. Purchasing a used chariot from Edvardus Fastus ("Fast Eddie") proved to be his first mistake (underpowered, only two horses when it needed four).

After making various new-camper mistakes, including the display of disgusting campground behavior and road-hogging that angered his fellow campers and chariot drivers, he fell into the clutches of a clever gypsy, who wanted to sell a glittering red wagon with yellow wheels.

Now Julius was paying the price for trading up with a twenty-year contract of "easy" payments.

Unfortunately, Julius had no money, so he was obliged to make payments in labor. After six months of manure shoveling, it finally dawned upon Julius that although he had a gorgeous rig with all the bells and whistles, he wasn't getting to use it very much. In fact, he had hitched up the four beautiful white horses to his magnificent red wagon with yellow wheels only twice for overnight trips to a nearby village where, because he had no money, he parked on the Gaul-Mart lot.

Realizing that he was spending his life working to pay for something that he didn't have the time and wherewithal to enjoy, Julius knew he had to get out of the pickle he was in. He had only two choices: Create more income to pay his debt or scale down his prized possession. Since he had no part-time job, he realized that he would have to give up his beautiful red wagon with yellow wheels and his powerful white horses.

Wily Roma and his band were the only chariot dealers in the village, so Julius turned to his creditor in desperation, seeking succor from his desperate circumstances. Because Wily had an enormous advantage over the simple Roman, Julius again came out a loser. Although the chariot and horses Julius had traded in on the red wagon had a Blue Scroll value of MX gold coins when the trade occurred, Wily offered him a beat-up chariot and one skinny horse worth only MI for his equity. Utterly defeated, Julius took the deal, thinking it was the only way to get out of the remaining 1,912 years of his contract.

The next morning, the dejected Julius packed his meager belongings, hitched up the skinny horse to the dilapidated chariot, called his faithful dog, Canis Sleepus, and once again hit the road. Typical of his disregard for the future, he didn't bother to examine his rig before taking off.

Only a couple of miles down the road, Julius's first mechanical failure occurred: A wheel fell off his chariot. Of course, he had no jack or other tools to make the repairs, so, not knowing what else to do, Julius just sat on a nearby log with his chin in his hands and felt sorry for himself. Canis Sleepus dognapped nearby.

Fortunately for the inept Roman, a wagon came by with a driver who took literally one of the basic tenets of the Bon Samaritan logo on his rig: Help Those in Distress. Pulling his steeds to a halt, he greeted the crestfallen Julius with a smile, a handshake, and an offer to help reattach the wheel.

Taking a jack from the large toolbox on the side of his wagon, the Bon Samaritan crawled under Julius's chariot and soon had the axle raised to the proper level to reattach the wheel. Noting that the wheel had fallen off due to the fact that the axle had no grease on it, he brought from his toolbox a clay pot of lard, which he liberally smeared on the axle and inside the hub before replacing the wheel.

After doing his good deed, the Bon Samaritan, in a kind and gentle fashion, suggested that Julius pay more attention to the maintenance of his rig.

Also noting that Julius's horse appeared to be in less-than-perfect condition, he urged Julius to do some maintenance in that regard. He suggested feeding the horse better and giving it adequate rest. He also suggested that Julius keep a record of what and when maintenance was done for future reference.

With his rig in travel-worthy condition, Julius again took to the road with a vow to always keep his axles greased and to obtain some basic tools to carry at all times. Even though he knew he wasn't very skilled at chariot repair, he realized that there were good folks out there who would help him in times of trouble. And that gave him a warm feeling about his fellow campers.

■ ■ ■

July 1997

Knowing When to Quit

T he prospect of having to give up driving a motorhome is not
a pleasant one, but it is a reality that faces every one of us. At
some point, we all stop RVing. Most of us voluntarily turn
in the keys at what seems to be an appropriate time; that is, when we
feel that the time has come. On the other hand, there are those of us
who must be forced to quit by their spouses or kids. It's a hard thing for
them to do, but sometimes there's no other way.

Recently a good friend of mine quit the hard way. His son simply took
the keys after trying to explain to his dad that his time had come. Although
my friend was an excellent longtime motorhome driver, a stroke a couple of years ago had left him somewhat impaired both mentally and physically. According to his wife, last year's long summer trek left her a nervous
wreck after her husband's poor reaction times forced three vehicles—
including a semi—off the road. She flatly refused to accompany him again
despite his protests that he was doing okay. In short, the son took her side
and the motorhome is up for sale. Tough love!

Another old friend of mine came to the conclusion on his own
that he couldn't handle his rig well enough to be out on the highway,
so he sold it. Now he and his wife live in a park-model trailer in an
RV park where the ambiance is what he has been accustomed to for
many years. In his upper seventies, he decided that his reaction times
weren't adequate for the demands of maneuvering a seven-ton motorhome in today's traffic. Smart man.

On the other hand, I have octogenarian friends who are convinced
that their driving abilities are not impaired by their advanced ages. Maybe
so, but I have my doubts. We may think that we drive as well as we did

when we were much younger, but in most cases that, unfortunately, is not the reality. I do believe that most of us who are very definitely seniors exercise more caution than we did when we were younger. That probably makes us less susceptible to some types of accidents. However, it is the ability and speed with which we identify potential problems and react to them that make a big difference in accident prevention. And the facts are simply that this is an area where age makes a difference.

Although we may be blind to our driving weaknesses, other people on the highway aren't. Unfortunately, due to their size, motorhomes (and their drivers) are very conspicuous to others, and our errors are compounded in their eyes. The driver of a car who is forced to take evasive action to keep from being hit by a motorhome doesn't see just another vehicle with just another driver. He sees "a darned old fool who ought not to be driving that big monster." And he lumps all silver-haired motorhome drivers in that category. Such judgments may not be fair, but they are often the reality.

So, what's the lesson here for those of us who fit the silver-haired-motorhome-driver category? Probably the first is to accept the fact that, as we get older, we must be more conscious of how we drive and be prepared to make adjustments as necessary. For example, night driving may have to be curtailed, big-city traffic avoided, steep and curvy mountain roads bypassed, and speed reduced. More than anything, we need to be more alert to where we are and what we are doing, that is, pay attention to our driving.

A second thing that we should do is pay more attention to what others are telling us about our driving, particularly our spouses. I jokingly say that I don't need to think about when I will quit driving our motorhome, because Margie will tell me and that will be that. I do pay attention to what she says. After all, she is there, she sees it all. I might tell myself that I'm still a great driver, but I can't kid her. Fortunately, I also believe her, so if and when she says "enough," it will be enough.

Lest readers think that I've become anti-old folks, think again. The facts are that as a group, we have marvelous driving records (ask your insurance man). And we also have the motorhomes. Unfortunately, the average age for a motorhome owner is around sixty. Very simply, most young people can't afford to purchase motorhomes, so a high proportion of RV owners are in the silver-haired category. Since we are the owners and drivers, we have a responsibility to other drivers not to be a real threat to them—which includes quitting when the time is right.

■ ■ ■